BIRDS

of NORTH AMERICA

Tom Wood, Sheri Williamson, and Jeffrey Glassberg

STERLING

New York / London

www.sterlingpublishing.com

STERLING and the distinctive Sterling logo are
registered trademarks of Sterling Publishing Co., Inc.

2   4   6   8   10   9   7   5   3   1

Published by Sterling Publishing Co., Inc.
387 Park Avenue South, New York, NY 10016

Distributed in Canada by Sterling Publishing
c/o Canadian Manda Group, 165 Dufferin Street
Toronto, Ontario, Canada M6K 3H6

Distributed in the United Kingdom by GMC Distribution Services
Castle Place, 166 High Street, Lewes, East Sussex, England BN7 1XU

Distributed in Australia by Capricorn Link (Australia) Pty. Ltd.
P.O. Box 704, Windsor, NSW 2756, Australia

Sterling ISBN 978-1-4027-8276-3

For information about custom editions, special sales, premium and
corporate purchases, please contact Sterling Special Sales
Department at 800-805-5489 or specialsales@sterlingpublishing.com.

American Bird Conservancy

American Bird Conservancy (ABC) is a nonprofit membership organization whose mission is to conserve wild birds and their habitats throughout the Americas. It is the only United States-based group dedicated solely to overcoming the greatest threats facing birds in the Western Hemisphere. ABC unites people and organizations around science-based approaches to priority issues through networks that include the Bird Conservation Alliance, North American Bird Conservation Initiative, Alliance for Zero Extinction, Partners in Flight, National Pesticide Reform Coalition, and a growing collaborative of international partners. Goals are accomplished through land acquisition, habitat restoration, and advocacy for improved policy and regulations. For more information, visit our website: www.abcbirds.org, or call 540-253-5780.

Contents

Above: American Goldfinch. **Opposite:** Black-capped Chickadee.

The World of Birds

*B*irds are everywhere, and although the pursuit of birds can take you to wild and remote places, all you really have to do to enjoy birds is to look around you. Peregrine Falcons hunt the skyscraper canyons of our big cities and American Robins share our yards and city parks from coast to coast. From inner city playgrounds to remote mountaintops, birds are a visible link to the natural world. An awareness of birds will allow you to tune in to the rhythms of a larger reality, one that marks seasons not by numbers on a calendar but by migration and song.

This book is intended as an introduction to the world of birds, with a focus on those regularly found in the Lower 48 states of the United States. Most of the more than seven hundred species of birds regularly found north of Mexico fall into distinct groups, and the first step in learning more about a bird is to place it into one of these groups. The majority of this book is devoted to introducing the major groups with basic aspects of their appearance, lifestyles, and habitats. Some of these groups have so few members that you should be able to identify your sighting to species. With more diverse groups, however, identification to species becomes more complicated. For example, you should be able to use this book to decide if that long-necked, gray bird is a crane or a heron. A gray crane is almost certainly a Sandhill Crane, but a gray heron may be a Great Blue Heron, a Tricolored Heron, or even a Reddish Egret. If, after experience, you decide that you would like to identify birds to specific species, even in difficult groups, then you can use other field guides that are designed for that purpose. For convenience, the groups are listed here in approximately the same order as they appear in most field guides, from the more primitive birds such as loons to the highly advanced songbirds.

Birds are everywhere, even in our major cities. Flocks of Snow Geese and Brant spend the winter at the Jamaica Bay unit of Gateway National Recreation Area in New York City, a short distance from the skyscraper canyons of Manhattan.

Birding

Bird watching, or birding, has grown from an esoteric pursuit of a few eccentrics to become one of the most popular outdoor activities in America, second only to gardening. Recent surveys have found that more than 60 million Americans watch birds, with more than 20 million traveling specifically for this purpose. This popularity dwarfs that of more "mainstream" hobbies such as golf or skiing, yet because birding is so often combined with other, better-known outdoor activities such as gardening, hiking, camping, and RVing, it goes largely unnoticed by the uninitiated. Not surprisingly, the media have not yet caught up to the expanded public interest in birds. Despite the larger demographic, the weekly migration report or rare bird alert has yet to join the ski and fishing reports on weekend newscasts.

Birding continues to grow in popularity, as shown by a 155 percent increase in numbers between 1983 and 1995. As the baby boomer generation ages, many are looking for gentle outdoor pursuits that can involve the whole family and, with the easy availability of birding resources and equipment, birding is an ideal activity. Part of the allure of birding is that it can be done with relatively little equipment; a pair of binoculars and a field guide are all you need to get started. That is not to underestimate the economic impact of birding. Even a small amount of equipment multiplied by 60 million birders is significant, and with travel and related expenses for the focused birder, fancy scopes, bird seed, and bird feeders for the backyard, the total expenditures

Above: Spotting scopes at the ready, a group of serious birders hits the beach.

Right: Although many of our beaches are shared by people and birds (in this case skimmers and terns), human activities are often incompatible with bird activities.

for birding is more than $30 billion. The growing popularity of birding has not gone completely unnoticed by marketers. There has been a corresponding growth in "bird stores" offering everything from bird seed (a more than $2-billion industry) to binoculars, birding apparel, and other accessories. Birding magazines, birding festivals, and even birding competitions have appeared in the last fifteen years as birding moves closer and closer to the mainstream.

One of the appeals of birding is that it can be enjoyed on so many levels. For many, simply noticing and appreciating the birds in their own backyards is enough. Most of these people would not consider themselves "bird watchers," yet they watch birds. Homeowners who buy bags of birdseed to attract a few birds to their yards are bird watchers. Hikers who carry binoculars along to enjoy the passing hawks are bird watchers. Because the term "bird watcher" carried some negative

Birders (and birds) are fortunate to have the outstanding National Wildlife Refuge system. Found throughout the United States, the many refuges are excellent places to visit to see and enjoy birds. Here, a group visits Great Dismal Swamp National Wildlife Refuge in Virginia.

connotations, those who take the hobby seriously prefer to be called by the more active-sounding term "birder." Many keep lists of species they have seen, from yard lists and year lists to country lists and life lists. While a casual birder in most parts of the country can see as many as two hundred different species of birds in his or her area, those interested in building up a larger and larger life list become more focused. Careful planning of vacations for the peak of migration or to areas with specific bird species becomes necessary. To see more than six hundred of the approximately eight hundred species found in North America, a birder must travel offshore on pelagic trips looking for oceangoing birds and to Alaska as well as to the birding hot spots of Texas, Florida, California, and Arizona. Some birders have built even larger lists with patience, travel, and a commitment to drop everything when a rare bird appears anywhere in the United States.

Most birders are more than willing to share sightings, tips, and expertise with novices, and meeting other birders at recognized "hot spots" or joining an organized group are good ways to get involved in birding. Although large groups are seldom conducive to good birding, under certain conditions the birds themselves attract a crowd. The hawk watch platform at Cape May State Park in New Jersey has been expanded several times to accommodate the crowds that gather each fall to watch the spectacle of thousand of hawks passing overhead, concentrated by the funnel effect of the Cape May Peninsula. Here is an opportunity to learn from the experts the subtleties of hawk identification while the throngs of birds overhead take little or no notice of the crowds of admirers below.

Beyond providing a healthy, wholesome outdoor recreational pursuit for millions of Americans, birding often leads to a broader and deeper interest in all aspects of the environment. For some, other wildlife that was previously overlooked takes on new importance. It is nearly impossible to study birds and not become an advocate for conservation. Bird lovers contribute millions of dollars and hundreds of thousands of hours of volunteer time to environmental organizations and public lands agencies. Given their numbers, birders, if mobilized, could become a political force to be reckoned with. Birding is also unique in the opportunity for an educated amateur to make real contributions to science. Legions of dedicated volunteers participate in a variety of citizen science activities from organized censuses to tracking of banded and marked birds.

The Audubon Christmas Bird Count is the largest volunteer monitoring effort of its type in the world. It began as a reaction to the tradition of the "Christmas Side Hunt." Prior to 1900, communities would often vie with each other to see which community could kill the most wildlife in a day. In 1900 the fledgling National Audubon Society, concerned about already declining bird numbers, proposed that instead of a hunt, a simple count of the birds in the area would be conducted. Since then the Christmas Bird Count has continued and expanded until more than 50,000 volunteers, counting in nearly two thousand "count circles," counted more than 63 million birds in 2004. By repeating the same counting techniques in the same area year after year, the data collected takes on scientific significance and can show long term trends in bird populations. Backyard bird counts and Cornell Laboratory of Ornithology's Project Feederwatch are other activities that give enthusiasts a chance to make a contribution to our understanding of our birds and their populations.

How to Watch Birds

RESOURCES

Getting started in bird watching is easier now than ever before. A wide and growing range of tools and resources are available, from lightweight, close-focusing binoculars and digital cameras to computerized identification aids and record-keeping software. The Audubon societies, bird clubs, and bird observatories, long the primary sources of local and regional information, now have websites that reach millions and offer instant access to information on sightings, identification, conservation issues, volunteer opportunities, and more. Internet forums and e-mail discussion

Land-water interfaces are always worth visiting. Migrating shorebirds are most easily seen on beaches and shorelines. Herons and egrets reside mainly along the water's edges, in marshes, swamps, seashores, and lakeshores. ***Above:*** A flock of White Ibis contrasts with the blue ocean on Big Pine Key, Florida.

groups have created a global community of bird lovers. Of course, you don't have to take advantage of the latest technology to enjoy birds. Some people get along without even the basic equipment, but a field guide, such as this one, and binoculars are a minor investment that help you get the most out of your birding experience.

A group of Utah birders takes the relaxed approach to birding, waiting for the birds to come to them.

A field guide is essential if you want to identify birds. There are many guides that cover the entire continental United States and Canada or divide the continent into eastern and western regions. There are also field guides that cover smaller areas, including single states: these vary widely in quality and are most useful if combined with guides of broader geographic scope. Specialty guides narrow the possibilities even further to just one group of birds. Birds of prey, hummingbirds, warblers, sparrows, shorebirds, and seabirds all have their own guides (sometimes more than one), and more such guides are on the way.

The illustrations in a field guide are important, but don't ignore the text and maps. Often the text gives crucial details about habitat, voice, or behavior, characteristics you can't discern from photographs or paintings alone. Traditional range maps depict normal breeding and wintering ranges. As more information has become available on bird distribution, range maps in field guides have become more complex, with new colors and symbols to represent relative abundance, migration routes, and locations of rare occurrence for the species. Reviewing the colors and symbols in the legend will help you interpret even the most complicated range maps.

Travel makes birding even more exciting, especially if you know where to find the best opportunities. Many states and regions now have guides to birding and wildlife viewing to help you locate the specific habitats and viewing areas. Scaled-down versions of these guides are often available for organized tour routes known as "birding trails." Birding trail projects typically involve government agencies, conservation organizations, and chambers of commerce. Links to sources for bird-finding guides and birding trail information are listed in the Bibliography.

EQUIPMENT

Binoculars can be a sizeable investment, but there are plenty of alternatives to taking out a second mortgage to buy the latest in birding optics. Many people start with hunting or stadium binoculars, retrieved from the attic or purchased at garage or estate sales. Unfortunately, these models are often unnecessarily heavy and lack the close-focus capability (less than ten feet) that is especially important for feeder watching. Mail-order companies and Internet auctions are other sources for birding optics, but buying binoculars sight unseen can be a waste of time and money. The best way to find a binocular that suits your eyes and your budget is to try out a few pairs. Optics manufacturers and retailers often have booths at birding festivals, and stores catering to birders usually have a few models selected especially for birding. Most birders use binoculars that are seven to ten power, meaning that the image is magnified seven to ten times. Binoculars with more than ten times magnification are difficult to hold steady and have a narrow field of view, which makes it difficult to locate the desired bird. Moderately priced binoculars in the $200–400 range are well worth the extra investment over discount store inexpensive ones. As in any hobby, those who must have the very best must be prepared to pay the price.

A spotting scope can be useful in many circumstances and, for serious birders, is almost essential for viewing and identifying seabirds and shorebirds. Unfortunately, high-quality scopes are still quite expensive and are cumbersome to carry around.

Checklists are a helpful tool for understanding the distribution of birds over time and space. They range from simple lists of birds seen at a particular location to in-depth summaries of decades of sightings. A good start for backyard birders is a checklist of the birds seen in your city, county, or state. This will help you keep records of which birds you see and, when you are trying to identify a bird, the checklist will narrow the list of likely candidates. Traditionally, checklists are printed as a brochure or booklet, although many are now online where they can be updated more easily.

Even if you limit your birding excursions to within a few miles of home, a bird-finding guide will be helpful. These guides, usually (but not always) written by local experts, are travel guides for finding the best birding locations. In addition to national and state parks, forest preserves, wildlife refuges, and nature centers, local bird-finding guides often mention urban parks, botanic gardens, cemeteries, marinas, wastewater facilities, landfills, private feeding stations, and even military installations — any place where birds congregate and birders are allowed to visit.

Local and regional organizations can help you with questions about identification, migration, backyard feeding, helping injured and orphaned birds, and dealing with nuisance birds. Many Audubon societies, bird observatories, and other nonprofit bird conservation organizations also offer field trips, workshops, and volunteer opportunities that can help you expand your horizons.

Wilderness areas, such as the Green River Trailhead in the Wind River Mountains of Wyoming, can provide exceptionally satisfying birding experiences. This area is home to Sandhill Cranes and many other species.

Finding Birds

WHERE TO FIND BIRDS

Certain habitats support more bird life than do others and these habitats will be more productive for birders as well. Wetlands are particularly important, providing nesting, wintering, and migratory stopover sites for birds of many species. Isolated patches of forest or woodland and narrow strips of vegetation along rivers, streams, and lakeshores often concentrate migrating birds.

An awareness of how the changing seasons affect birds is vital in planning a birding adventure. Spring and early summer, when many birds are wearing their breeding finery and when singing and courtship are at their peak, are perhaps the best times to go afield. Late summer and early fall are also excellent, especially for observing parents and their young as well as tackling shorebirds, flycatchers, fall warblers, immature hummingbirds, and other identification challenges. Winter can also be a good time for birding, especially in the milder southern climates.

Birding is, in many ways, analogous to hunting, perhaps even tapping into the same primal instincts. The keys to finding birds are to put yourself in the proper habitat, pay attention to motion and sound, and not disturb your quarry. The best birders, like the best hunters, move quietly in the woods, stopping often to listen and watch. This low-key, patient approach is especially important when searching for wary species that flee or hide at the first sign of an intruder. Loud noises and sudden movements will alert the birds to your presence and reduce your chances of seeing them. Since birds have good color vision, it is best not to wear white or bright colors while birding. Muted browns, greens, and grays are preferred for field attire.

Although you can probably see more than three hundred kinds of birds near where you live, if you want to see more species of birds you will need to travel across the country and to the borders. Many species, including strays from Mexico, can be seen at the Santa Ana National Wildlife Refuge in extreme southern Texas (**top**) and in Sycamore Canyon in Santa Cruz County, Arizona (**right**).

Some birds are quite easy to see, seemingly confident in their ability to escape any danger that presents itself. Others are too shy to sit in plain view but reveal their presence with songs or calls. For most of us, the call or song of a bird simply focuses our attention toward a particular bush or tree, but many experienced birders are able to identify birds by their sounds and do more birding by ear than with binoculars. It's possible to turn the tables on birds and lure them out of hiding using a soft pishing sound similar to their common alarm calls.

ETHICS

Although we think of birding as a "non-consumptive" recreational activity, it is not without impact on birds and their habitats. With the myriad hazards facing our birds today and with the growing popularity of birding, birders have a responsibility to minimize the effects our recreational activities have on birds and their environment. We also have an obligation to be courteous and considerate of other birders and non-birders, and not inconvenience other recreationists, landowners, or neighbors. To promote the welfare of birds and goodwill toward birders, the American Birding Association, an organization of recreational birders, has adopted a code of ethics based on these principles (see www.americanbirding.org/abaethics.htm for more information).

Bird Feeding

One easy way to maximize your birding experience is by inviting birds to your own yard. Bird feeding provides an opportunity to bring the birds to you so you can watch them at your leisure. By simply providing birds with their basic needs — food, water, and shelter — you can make your home a haven for a variety of birds.

SEED

A quick perusal of the group accounts in this book shows just how many groups of birds are adapted to eating seeds. Finches, grosbeaks, sparrows, quail, doves, and others are specialists in eating seeds and can readily be attracted to seeds in your yard. You can even influence which birds come to your yard by the type of seed that you provide. Sunflower seeds, in particular the small black oil variety, are the favorite of many of our most popular feeder birds. Chickadees, titmice, jays, and cardinals all love sunflower seeds. For a more varied clientele, use a mix with tiny millet seeds which are preferred by some of the smaller sparrows and finches. Any seed mix you purchase should list sunflower seed and millet as the primary ingredients. By contrast, some of the "less desirable" species that frequent bird feeders (pigeons, house sparrows, and cowbirds) often prefer the large red milo seeds that often are a major component, as filler, of cheap seed mixes. Unless you are trying to attract quail, native doves, or some other large species to your yard, it is best to avoid these seeds and the mixes that contain them.

Often the best seed mixes can be found at feed stores and specialty bird stores where custom mixes for the birds in your area may be offered. Other menu items might include safflower, a hard-coated seed that cardinals and a few other large-billed birds can use. It may take a while for your cardinals to learn to eat safflower seed, but you won't be feeding your House Sparrows in the meantime. Nyjer (also spelled "niger") seed is a tiny seed preferred by goldfinches. Often erroneously called "thistle," this oily, black seed is expensive and best fed in a special feeder with small openings accessible only to the thin bills of goldfinches and siskins.

SUET

Suet is a hard fat that can provide nutrition for many species of birds, including some that may not visit seed feeders. Woodpeckers, mockingbirds, and orioles frequently come to suet feeders. Suet can be obtained from a butcher shop and hung by itself or in wire cages but is also sold in cake form at bird specialty stores. Look for the suet dough mixes, which are less likely to melt away on warm days. Fancy suet cakes may contain fruit, peanut butter, or other ingredients to appeal to a wider range of tastes and nutritional needs.

WATER

One of the best ways to attract birds to your yard is by providing a water source. It can be as simple as a shallow tray of water functioning as a basic bird bath or as elaborate as a re-circulating stream and waterfall. Moving water seems to have a particular attraction for birds, and even a simple drip arrangement will draw more attention to your water feature. Many birds that would not otherwise

Above left: Flamboyant Pileated
Woodpeckers, the models for Woody
Woodpecker, would be large (the size of
crows), spectacular additions to your feeder
birds. Here one enjoys suet. **Above right:**
Fruits add important nutrients to the diets of
many birds, including Northern Flickers.
Right: Black nyjer seeds are especially suited
to small finches such as American Goldfinches.
Because these oily, black seeds are quite
expensive, you probably want to serve them
in a special feeder that only allows access to
birds with small bills.

be attracted by food will come to a yard
providing water, particularly in the drier
parts of the country. Keep the bird bath
clean with regular maintenance. In
northern climes, a heater may be required
to keep the water from freezing. Birds must bathe often, even in winter, to maintain the insulating
properties of their feathers, so a water feature provides more than just a drink for your birds.

Hummingbirds and flowers were meant for each other. Ruby-throated Hummingbirds, shown above, are found throughout much of the eastern United States.

ATTRACTING HUMMINGBIRDS

These living jewels are easy to attract to a garden by planting flowers and shrubs that provide food and shelter. A local nursery can advise you as to which flowers are hummingbird attractors and can be grown in your area. A variety of commercial hummingbird feeders in a dizzying array of styles and sizes are also available. Look for one that is easy to fill and clean. Keeping the feeder clean and filled with a mixture of sugar and water (one part sugar to four parts water) to mimic the natural flower nectars is the secret to attracting hummingbirds. There is no need to add red food coloring or use commercial products containing these and other potentially harmful chemicals. At best, hummingbird feeders mimic natural food sources, and in nature the flowers are red but the nectar is colorless. Refined table sugar has a bad reputation, but for hummingbirds the pure sucrose of white sugar closely approximates the sugars found in flower nectars. Never use artificial sweeteners or honey in an artificial nectar mix. Keep the feeders clean and supplied with fresh sugar water and you may soon have a yard full of hummingbirds. Hummingbirds can be very territorial, and an array of feeders, some out of sight of one another, will allow several birds to peacefully feed in your yard simultaneously.

While hummingbird feeders are a great way to bring the birds to your yard so you can enjoy watching them, they do not provide a complete diet. Hummingbirds also need insects to provide the nutrients lacking in nectar or sugar water, so a pesticide-free yard is also a necessity. Feeders will not short-circuit the hummingbirds' natural instinct to migrate. You can take the feeders down in the fall after the birds leave your area, but leaving them up will not entice the birds to forego migration.

FEEDER MAINTENANCE AND TROUBLESHOOTING

Well-designed feeders can reduce the drudgery of feeder maintenance. Optional seed-catching trays reduce waste and mess, and clear plastic domes keep seed dry while maintaining your view of the action. Nevertheless, regular cleaning is vital to prevent the spread of disease among your clientele. A good cleaning kit begins with stiff-bristled brushes of various sizes, from narrow bottle brushes for feeder ports to long-handled scrub brushes for bird baths. Plain water is the easiest and safest cleaning agent, but feeders can be disinfected by soaking in a solution of one part chlorine bleach in ten parts water and rinsing well. Seed feeders must dry thoroughly before refilling to prevent toxic mold from growing inside. Monthly cleaning is adequate for seed feeders, but hummingbird and oriole feeders require thorough cleaning every two to four days (more often in hot weather).

Though many backyard bird enthusiasts welcome all comers to their feeding stations, some species can wear out their welcome rather quickly. Some people view non-native species such as Rock Pigeons, European Starlings, and House Sparrows as unwanted feeder visitors. Pigeons are a frequent nuisance in urban areas, and the mess produced by a big flock hanging around your feeders can cause serious problems with your human neighbors. House Sparrows are noisy and build their messy nests in nooks and crannies on buildings as well as in dense shrubbery. They also take over nest boxes intended for bluebirds and Purple Martins. Some native birds may also be considered a nuisance at feeders, especially large species such as doves and jays that tend to intimidate smaller birds. Discouraging problem birds may be as simple as using the right feeders or as drastic as withholding feed for days or weeks until the offenders give up and move on. Your local nature center, bird observatory, or store catering to birders can offer suggestions on reducing or eliminating these problems.

Feeding stations often provide food for more than just seed-eating birds. Hawks often find the crowds of distracted prey easy pickings. The most common birds of prey to haunt feeding stations are the Cooper's and Sharp-shinned hawks, short-winged forest raptors adapted to hunt birds. Seeing a hawk snag a favorite songbird from a feeder can be emotionally devastating, but hawks are equally interesting and valuable creatures in their own right. Hawk problems are usually self limiting; as prey species become warier and their visits to the feeders less frequent, the hawk will become discouraged and move on in search of more productive hunting grounds. If you feel you must do something, the most effective remedy is to stop feeding for a few days to a couple of weeks until the hawk has relocated.

One bird that should never be welcome at feeding stations is the Brown-headed Cowbird. This native blackbird is a brood parasite, laying its eggs in the nests of other birds. The impact that cowbirds have on the nesting success of songbirds such as thrushes, warblers, vireos, and tanagers is magnified when the female cowbirds have an abundant food supply with which to produce eggs. If your feeder attracts cowbirds, discontinue feeding lest you do more harm than good for the local birds.

Birds are not the only visitors to bird feeders. Squirrels are the most familiar of the furry feeder marauders, but in more rural areas foxes, deer, and even bears may take advantage of the food you provide. Large mammals that become habituated to humans are a public safety issue and must be discouraged before they become a danger to people and pets. As with larger birds, the most effective approach to discouraging mammals is to use the right feeders and clean up spilled seed promptly.

The Nature of Birds

FORMED FOR FLIGHT

Throughout human history, the gift we have most admired — and most envied — in birds is their ability to fly. Although some birds are flightless or fly very little, adaptations for life in the air have played the greatest role in shaping birds from their earthbound dinosaur ancestors into the richly varied creatures we see today.

Part of the equation necessary for flight is a powerful engine. The muscular, respiratory, and circulatory systems of birds are all super-charged compared to those of mammals. Huge breast muscles attached to a narrow keeled breastbone power the wings. In strong fliers, such as most songbirds, these muscles are rich in blood vessels supplied by a four-chambered heart that may be twice as large as that of a mammal of similar size. Minimizing weight is the second part of the flight equation, and the anatomy of birds takes this to amazing extremes. Birds' bones are hollow, filled with air spaces that add to the efficiency of the respiratory system while providing light, strong support for the muscles. A Magnificent Frigatebird with a seven-foot wingspan has a skeleton that weighs only about four ounces — less than its feathers.

Flight style and speed vary greatly depending on lifestyle. The Peregrine Falcon, generally considered the fastest of all birds, is capable of reaching speeds of more than two hundred miles per hour when stooping at prey. Its lungs would explode from the inrushing air if not for baffles in its nostrils. Swallows are graceful fliers but have little need for speed; they seldom exceed twenty miles per hour. Many birds of prey save energy by taking advantage of rising air currents. This behavior can be seen especially well during fall migration, as thousands of southbound

Birds are made to fly! A frigatebird (**right**), with a wingspan that is longer than a man is tall, has a skeleton that weighs only about four ounces and a total weight of only two to three pounds. Many birds can reach flying speeds of more than seventy-five miles per hour and some falcons and swifts can reach two hundred miles per hour. Although most flight is relatively close to the ground, migrating birds often fly very high and some birds have collided with airplanes at more than 30,000 feet above the ground.

Owls, such as this Western Screech-Owl, must move their heads to focus on an object because the very large, forward-facing eyes of owls are immobile. In addition, although owl eyes are superb at light-gathering, they have a very narrow field of view. When you scan a field with binoculars, your view is closer to an owl's vision than when you use only your eyes.

hawks ride updrafts along mountain ridges and bubbles of warm air rising from open ground. The extremely long, narrow wings of seabirds such as albatrosses enable them to glide a few inches above the water on wind currents deflected from the surfaces of waves. Kingfishers, some small songbirds, and a few birds of prey can remain stationary for a few wingbeats, but hummingbirds are masters of hovering flight. Quail and grouse are mainly ground birds, but when threatened they explode upward in a blur of wings before gliding to safety nearby.

UNCOMMON SENSES

To maneuver deftly in three dimensions a bird needs excellent vision and reflexes. In the majority of birds, the eyes take up most of the skull, and the optic lobes occupy most of the brain. Diurnal birds have excellent color vision, and some species see in greater detail than humans do. Retinas that are tightly packed with receptor cells enable a Golden Eagle to see a rabbit from over a mile away. Colored oil droplets in the eyes of some seabirds act like polarizing sunglasses, cutting glare to reveal prey just below the surface. The large, forward-facing eyes of owls are superb at gathering light, enabling the birds to hunt in near darkness. Barn Owls take night hunting a step further, with unique asymmetrical ear openings that allow them to triangulate and locate prey by sound alone, even in complete darkness.

Smell is one sense that is much less developed in birds than it is in mammals. Turkey Vultures are among the few birds known to use smell to locate food, often following the scent of carrion upwind. While a bird's sense of smell is limited, this can be an advantage. For example, Great Horned Owls are oblivious to the chemical defenses of skunks and regularly take them as prey.

In addition to providing warmth and protection, feathers can serve as whiskers, as on the Common Poorwill (**top left**). Color patterns of feathers can help camouflage birds. The Long-eared Owl (**above right**) blends into the tree branches, while the black belly and variegated topside of the Pacific Golden-Plover (**bottom left**) can make it look like a patch of tundra grass.

FEATHERS

Feathers are the primary defining characteristic of birds. A bird's covering of feathers, also known as plumage, protects the body from environmental extremes and streamlines it for flight. Individual feathers also serve many different purposes. Birds that catch insects on the wing often have sensory "whiskers" around their mouths much like those of a cat. Members of the pigeon and heron families have down feathers that fragment into a waterproof powder used to groom the rest of the plumage. Feathers also serve as ornaments to impress the opposite sex, such as the lacy plumes of Snowy Egrets and the brilliant, coppery gorgets of male Rufous Hummingbirds. Some birds have specialized feathers that produce mechanical sounds used in territorial or courtship displays. In adult males of both the American Woodcock and Broad-tailed Hummingbird, the outermost flight feathers have narrow tips that create distinctive whistling sounds in flight.

Not all feathers are intended to draw attention. Birds that need to be inconspicuous usually have plumage colored and patterned to match their usual backgrounds. An incubating Mallard on her nest may look like just another pile of dead cattails to a passing predator. Owls wear some of nature's finest camouflage, which helps them avoid detection on their daytime roosts. At night, they take stealth a step further with soundproofing for silent flight. Even bold patterns can fool the eye of a predator, by breaking up the silhouette and making it unclear where the bird leaves off and the background begins.

Feathers typically are molted and re-grown once each year, though sometimes this occurs in stages that can complicate identification. Young birds are often much less colorful than adults, and it may take more than one molt for their plumage to reach maturity. It takes five years and

White-tailed Ptarmigans, found high in the Rockies, change their feathers between winter and summer; their white winter garb camouflages them on the snow, while their speckled summer-wear helps them to melt into lichen-covered rocks.

Beginning birders are sometimes confused by the different feather colors seen on the same bird species. Adult female Summer Tanagers (**top**) are greenish-yellow while adult males (**right**) are bright red. Males molting into adult breeding plumage (**bottom left**) are a patchwork of yellow and red.

Vireos and warblers are small, look-alike groups. A close and careful look at their bills allows one to recognize them as distinct. Vireo bills are slightly chunkier and shorter than are warbler bills and, unlike sharp-pointed warbler bills, are slightly hooked at the end. **Top left:** Red-eyed Vireo. **Top right:** Worm-eating Warbler. **Left:** Tennessee Warbler.

five molt cycles for Bald Eagles to acquire their striking white head and tail feathers. Even mature birds of many species undergo seasonal color changes. A few very colorful birds, including male dabbling ducks, Indigo Buntings, and American Goldfinches, molt at the end of the breeding season into a nondescript plumage that helps to make them inconspicuous to predators. A second molt cycle brings them back into full color before the next breeding season. The fact that a bird may not look the same year-round offers an additional challenge to beginning birders. Molting helps some non-migratory birds adapt to seasonal changes in their environment. A White-tailed Ptarmigan that lives above timberline in the Rocky Mountains is mottled brown in summer to match the tundra vegetation and white in winter to disappear against a background of snow.

FEEDING AND BILL ADAPTATIONS

Certain groupings in this book make particular mention of bill shape as a quick way to gain insight into the bird's ecological niche. The shape of a bird's bill is directly related to the type of food it eats. Some species have very specialized bills for particular feeding strategies. Unique bill shapes alone will allow you to identify Roseate Spoonbills (page 58) and American Avocets (page 106), and subtleties of bill shape are often the key to discriminating between similar groups of birds, such as vireos and warblers or sparrows and finches. The powerful, curved bill of an owl or falcon immediately identifies it as a bird of prey, while the long spear-like bill of a Great Blue Heron is an indicator of its fishing lifestyle.

Bird bills vary dramtically in size and shape and are adapted to different feeding strategies. **Above:** Great Blue Herons use their long, pointed bills to spear fish and occasionally other birds, such as Sora Rails. **Opposite page top:** A female Eastern Bluebird sizes up a choice berry. **Opposite bottom:** The curved and powerful bills of raptors, such as this Saw-whet Owl, are used to tear into their prey.

BEHAVIOR

Differences in behavior are helpful in identifying the group or species to which a bird belongs. For example, both woodpeckers and nuthatches are adept at climbing trees, but only nuthatches can reverse direction and climb head-down with equal ease. The nervous wing flicks of the kinglets help to separate them from the similar looking but more sedate vireos. Behavior-watching is also a great way to move beyond simple identification into a deeper understanding of the birds themselves. A Peregrine Falcon on a utility pole is a magnificent sight, but the same bird diving at a flock of shorebirds can elicit gasps from even the most experienced observer.

Opposite: A Great Egret shows off its finery during a courtship display. In the early 1900s, the rage for egret feathers as adornment for womens' hats, led to the decimation of egret colonies. The National Audubon Society was formed, in part, in response to the wanton killing. **Left:** Great Blue Herons go bill to bill, with feathers bristling. **Bottom:** Sharp-tailed Grouse gather in the spring. Groups of males perform courtship displays and dances to attract females. During the displays, male Sharp-tailed Grouse show off their pink neck patches (usually hidden under feathers) and thrust their tail feathers into the air to impress females.

COURTSHIP

Family life begins with courtship. Usually it is the male's responsibility to woo the female and fend off competing suitors, although a few species reverse these roles. Extravagant plumage and complex songs may serve as indicators of the physical fitness or experience of a suitor, helping prospective mates choose among many possible partners. In highly social birds such as cranes and geese, adolescents often gather in "bachelor flocks" in which they practice their social skills. Bonds that form in these flocks may grow into lifelong partnerships.

Each type of bird builds a nest that is characteristic of its species. **Opposite:** A male Baltimore Oriole admires his handiwork. **Above top:** A Hooded Warbler keeps the eggs warm. **Above bottom left:** American Robins typically lay three or four robin's-egg blue eggs per clutch. **Above bottom right:** Hummingbirds often use lichens and spiderwebs to make their tiny, carefully constructed nests.

NESTING

A bird's nest can be as simple as a bare rock ledge or as elaborate as the woven nests of orioles. Many nests are built for a single use, but others, particularly the bulky stick nests of hawks and eagles, are added to not only over multiple seasons but by successive generations. One of the largest Bald Eagle nests on record was used for thirty-six years before it was blown down in a

Some birds create nests in enclosures with a small opening. **Top:** Cliff Swallows use mud to form a protective bowl. ***Middle left:*** Woodpeckers create their own nesting holes by drilling into dead or decaying trees. Endangered Red-cockaded Woodpeckers require old-age southern pines. ***Middle right:*** Many hole-nesting birds, such as Tree Swallows, cannot make their own nest holes and use abandoned woodpecker holes or man-made boxes. ***Left:*** The decline in nest holes was one of the factors that led to a decline in bluebird populations. A concerted campaign to erect bluebird nesting boxes throughout much of the United States has again made bluebirds a common sight.

Successful nesting results in fledglings — young birds that have obtained their feathers and left the nest, but that still depend upon the parents. ***Overleaf:*** These young Ospreys, on their nest within sight of Manhattan, are almost ready to fly. Many hawks, eagles, and ospreys will use the same nest for many years. ***Above left:*** Left-leaning Barred Owl fledglings. ***Above right:*** A Great Horned Owl fledgling adopts a defensive posture.

storm. It measured eight and a half feet in diameter and twelve feet high and was estimated to weigh nearly two tons. In contrast, the female Calliope Hummingbird binds many layers of soft plant fibers with spiderwebs to create a thick-walled cup less than two inches across. Woodpeckers chisel their own nest cavities in trees, which helps to dismantle dead and diseased trees and recycle their nutrients back into the ecosystem. Many hole-nesting birds lack the tools for excavating nest cavities. These species depend on the abandoned nests of woodpeckers or natural cavities. Purple Martins and bluebirds are secondary cavity nesters that have received a great deal of attention because they will readily use nest boxes provided by their human admirers. Bluebird boxes helped to restore populations of these lovely birds in parts of the eastern states.

As a rule, a bird's nest is a nursery, not a home, but there are many exceptions. Cactus Wrens build enclosed nests, usually in cacti or thorny desert shrubs. While the female incubates, the male builds a secondary nest for roosting. Once the growing young begin to crowd the original nest interior, the female builds her own "bedroom" nearby. Flocks of Bushtits regularly roost together in their sock-like nests. During severe cold spells, more than a dozen Eastern Bluebirds may crowd into a single natural cavity or box used in summer for nesting.

FAMILY LIFE

All birds lay eggs, and the eggs must be kept safe and warm until they hatch. Beyond these fundamentals, the strategies that birds employ to ensure the future of their kind are almost as varied as the birds themselves. In some species, the relationship between male and female spans no more than a few minutes or hours, while in others the bond lasts for a lifetime. Even parental care varies widely. In cowbirds, neither parent takes responsibility for their young; the female simply places

her eggs in the care of other birds. Hummingbirds and most ducks have single parent families, with the female responsible for nest building, incubation, and care of the young. For many birds, the greatest nesting success is possible when both parents contribute to the welfare of the young. Eagles and cranes invest months in each offspring, from incubating the eggs to teaching the youngsters to fend for themselves. A few species take parenting to the next level — the previous year's young, other relatives, or even unrelated birds cooperate to raise a single brood. In some cases these "nest helpers" may wait years to raise their own young. They bring food to the nest, chase off predators, and may even help to incubate the eggs.

SONGS AND CALLS

Bird song is one of the most complex aspects of bird behavior. Although some species are nearly silent or make only nonmusical grunts, barks, or squeals, birds far exceed any other group of animals in their vocal artistry. Most apparently hatch with an instinctive template of their species-specific song that is refined through listening to their parents and other birds of their species. Just as in human speech, this results in regional dialects; a cardinal in New England will sound similar, but not identical, to a cardinal in Arizona. Males may sing to defend a territory or, in the case of nonterritorial species such as House Finches, simply to attract the attention of females. Some species are talented mimics, able to reproduce the sound of everything from the other birds in their habitat to car alarms and cell phones. Some evidence indicates

One of the great joys of birding is the exuberance and variety of bird songs. **Top:** This Eastern Meadowlark is most easily distinguished from a Western Meadowlark by its song. **Bottom:** Listening to a dawn chorus that includes many species of migrating warblers, such as this Blue-winged Warbler, is a thrilling experience.

that females select males who have a greater vocal repertoire over less talented rivals. Not all females are content to sit on the sidelines, and in some species mated pairs perform intricate duets.

Birds often sing from prominent perches, the better to advertise their presence to rivals or prospective mates. Some birds of open country even sing on the wing in a display known as "skylarking." Males of many familiar hummingbird species perform spectacular looping dive displays accompanied by unique vocal and mechanical sounds.

Calls are simpler and more commonly heard than songs. Even birds that have no true song usually have an array of simple, instinctive sounds used to warn off intruders, call attention to danger, beg for food, or express pain or fear. The distinction between songs and calls is one of function and complexity rather than aesthetics; as pleasing as they are to the human ear, the yodel of the Common Loon and the bugle of the Sandhill Crane are not considered songs.

MIGRATION

No aspect of bird behavior captures our imagination as much as migration. The ebb and flow of birds across the hemispheres is the pulse of the planet, connecting your backyard with the tropical forests of Central and South America. Birds are the earth's most visible migrants, but not all birds migrate. A Wrentit may live its entire twelve-year life within 1300 feet of where it hatched while other species, such as Northern Mockingbirds, move more widely but don't undertake true migrations. However,

Top: A Sage Thrasher sings its warbling song from the top of a bush, all the better to be seen and heard. The songs of most mockingbirds, catbirds, and thrashers are loud and varied, often mimicking other birds and other sounds from their environment. ***Bottom:*** Chestnut-sided Warbler.

Bird migration is the pulse of the planet, massively reshuffling life each spring and fall. During these migrations the birds may fly high — thousands of feet above ground. **Top left:** Flocks of American White Pelicans can appear almost anywhere in the continental United States. **Top right:** Young Blackpoll Warblers, born in Canada, migrate to South America. **Middle right:** Arctic Terns spend the summer in the Arctic and the winter in the Antarctic! **Bottom:** Many ducks, such as these Greater Scaup, migrate and spend the winter in large flocks.

some species perform amazing feats of navigation and endurance. The champion migrant is the Arctic Tern, which spends the summer in Arctic waters, then as winter approaches flies to the Antarctic for the southern summer.

The Bar-tail Godwit, a medium-sized shorebird that nests on the coast of Alaska, makes one of the most amazing journeys of any creature. As fall approaches, the adults depart for their wintering grounds, leaving the young birds to fatten up for their impending trip. A young godwit, normally weighing about twelve ounces, will gorge itself until it is about 55 percent fat, having reduced its entire digestive system to a fraction of the usual size before leaving on its marathon trip. With only a couple of weeks of flight practice and almost too fat to fly, the young birds take off and fly non-stop across open ocean to New Zealand. These youngsters have never seen New Zealand but instinctively know that a six-day non-stop flight on favorable winds will bring them to a safe winter haven.

Two other astounding migrations involve much smaller birds. The Blackpoll Warbler, weighing about half an ounce, flies across Canada to New England then out to sea, turning right and continuing to northeastern South America. Again, the young birds do not fly with their parents, but rely solely on instinct to guide them to their winter home. Ruby-throated Hummingbirds that visit gardens and feeders in the eastern United States each summer spend the winters in southern Mexico and Central America and fly from the Yucatan Peninsula over the Gulf of Mexico to our shores. The fall migration is more leisurely, curving around the Gulf coast through Texas and eastern Mexico to the wintering grounds.

Knowledge of migration routes and timing provides the opportunity for some wonderful birding experiences. In spring, arriving songbirds often congregate along the Gulf Coast. Exhausted by their long flight, they seek refuge in patches of woodland near the shore to rest and refuel before moving on. Recent advances in radar ornithology have allowed biologists to track waves of birds approaching the coast, revealing that under favorable conditions many birds move inland nearly a hundred miles before landing. Nevertheless, a spring birding trip planned to intercept the waves of migrants moving north can be a spectacular experience.

In fall migration, many birds are funneled into particular areas by geographic features. Updrafts off Hawk Mountain in Pennsylvania create an escalator in the sky, and thousands of birds of prey stream over the ridge tops each fall. In late September, tens of thousands of Ruby-throated Hummingbirds and Broad-winged Hawks follow the curve of the Texas coast southward toward Mexico. Farther south in Mexico, near the coastal city of Veracruz, mountains encroach on the coastal plain, creating a bottleneck in the migration route. On some fall days, over a million birds of prey pass overhead, an awesome spectacle that must be seen to be believed.

Migration is tangible evidence of the interconnectedness of the most remote reaches of the planet. Near our home in southeastern Arizona, it is possible, for a short while each fall and spring, to see a Swainson's Hawk that winters in the pampas of Argentina sharing a field with a Sandhill Crane that nests in the arctic wilderness of Siberia. Knowledge of these birds and their epic journeys adds greatly to the enjoyment of such an encounter.

Conservation

When the first Europeans arrived on the shores of North America, they found a continent teeming with almost unimaginable numbers of birds and other animals. They set about exploiting these wild populations, first for food, then for profit. Rare species that were particularly desirable as table fare went first. Among these was the lovely Labrador Duck, extinct by 1825. As the human population grew, even the most numerous birds were no match for the market gunners, who killed thousands of ducks, shorebirds, doves, pigeons, quail, and even songbirds to stock city meat markets. Despite early conservation efforts, our native bird populations declined. In 1781, laws were passed to try to protect the Heath Hen, a northeastern subspecies of the Greater Prairie-Chicken. By 1932 they were gone. In 1808, Alexander Wilson estimated one flock of Passenger Pigeons at 2.2 billion birds. Despite laws passed to protect the birds from market hunting, in less than one hundred years the last wild Passenger Pigeon was gone. Martha, the last Passenger Pigeon on earth, died in the Cincinnati Zoo in 1914 at the age of twenty-nine.

It was the plume trade that finally turned public opinion against commercial exploitation of our native birds. In the early days of the 20th century, decorating women's fashions with elegant feathers and even whole stuffed birds was all the rage. To satisfy demand for this avian finery, plume hunters sought the nesting colonies of herons and egrets and shot the adults as they returned to their nests. Their elegant nuptial plumes were ripped out, their bloody carcasses discarded, and their nestlings left to die. The National Audubon Society was born of the outrage over this cruel and senseless slaughter.

The Migratory Bird Treaty Act of 1918 was a landmark in conservation, protecting all birds except the birds of prey, which were then considered "varmints." Amendments gave full federal protection to all birds except for the non-migratory upland game birds (quail, grouse, turkey), whose management was left to the states. Nevertheless, the Bald Eagle, our national symbol since 1782, was widely persecuted as vermin until given protection by the Bald Eagle Act of 1940. With protection from shooting and the later banning of the pesticide DDT, which caused thinning of eggshells of these and other birds of prey, the Bald Eagle has recovered to the point where it has been considered for removal from the Endangered Species List.

In the group accounts that follow, we relate problems with specific birds and groups that should serve as a cautionary tale as we see the multitude of threats and concerns that face birds of all types. As birders, we can address some of the major threats that face many of our bird species through advocacy and volunteerism.

HABITAT

Foremost of the problems facing birds today is habitat loss. It has been compared to a life-and-death game of musical chairs, where each year returning migrants find the available habitat smaller than the year before, leaving some with nowhere to go. The issue is not simply having a tree in which to nest. As large forest tracts are fragmented, the resident birds are more susceptible to threats such as cowbird parasitism, feral cats, and other dangers not as prevalent in deep woods. Forest birds often have no innate defense against new perils. An additional challenge for conservation of migratory birds is that they require habitat in both their wintering areas and their nesting grounds as well as at critical layover points in between. For some, this means a deciduous woodland in the United States for the summer as well as a tropical forest for the winter. Conservation of migratory birds is an international effort, with prosperous countries aiding the efforts of developing nations to preserve our common natural heritage.

CATS

As more and more of our songbirds come in contact with suburbia, the problem of free-roaming pet cats and their feral counterparts becomes more significant. Nearly 40 million cats in the United States are allowed to roam free. The cats themselves face many dangers — an outdoor cat's life expectancy is half that of an indoor cat — but the toll they take on wildlife is staggering. A study sponsored by the University of Wisconsin estimated that rural cats kill 40 million birds a year in Wisconsin alone. With birds facing so many other hazards — from radio towers, high-rise windows, pesticides, and habitat loss — the addition of a non-native predator may be enough to push some species over the brink. The American Bird Conservancy has joined with the Humane Society of the United States, American Humane Association, Pet Care Trust, and other groups to encourage cat owners to save the lives of millions of cats and birds by keeping their pets indoors.

PESTICIDES

The use of many hazardous pesticides has been restricted or banned in the United States. Although agriculture still depends heavily on chemical use, a tenuous balance has been struck between pest control and environmental protection. Unfortunately, residues of some pesticides remain in soil and sediments for decades after their last application, and migratory birds often visit countries where banned chemicals are still in use. A recent incident in Argentina where more than six thousand Swainson's Hawks were killed by a poison sprayed to control grasshoppers serves as both a sobering wake-up call to the dangers of some of these poisons and also as a model of international cooperation. Scientists and conservationists from both Argentina and North America worked together with the farmers and the chemical company to recall the product and educate the public on its danger to the hawks. Thanks to these efforts, only twenty-four hawks died the following year.

Those inviting wildlife to their yards have a particular responsibility to ensure that they are not exposed to pesticides that can affect them. Growing insect- and disease-resistant plants and encouraging beneficial insects and spiders reduce both the need for chemicals and the drudgery of garden maintenance. A healthy population of birds is a gardener's greatest ally against insect pests and weeds.

Above: Yellow-crowned Night-Heron. ***Opposite:*** Purple Finch.

Species Guide

*T*he photographs and descriptions on the following pages are designed to enable you to identify almost any bird you see to one of the groups shown in each two-page treatment. The groups described in these treatments are not artificial constructs; rather each group is composed of very similar species that are more closely related to each other than they are to other birds.

The order in which the groups are presented is similar to that found in most recent field guides and, in general, progresses from groups believed to be "primitive" (that is, not much changed from an ancient group of birds) to those believe to be more recently evolved.

Names

The names used in this book follow those of the American Ornithologists' Union. Before the Information Age, the names of birds and other wildlife varied from place to place. A small song-bird known in one community as a "wild canary" might be called a "thistle bird" in another area and simply a "yellow bird" elsewhere. Biologists traditionally avoided such confusion by giving each species a two-part scientific name, usually with Latin or Greek roots. Though this system is useful for professionals communicating across language barriers, few amateurs are motivated to learn hundreds of Latinized names. Since the late 1950s, the American Ornithologists' Union has assigned each bird species in North America a single official English name, making birding and ornithology much more user friendly. Instead of struggling to remember *Carduelis tristis*, both ornithologists and birders can share information about the American Goldfinch. In recent years the increase in popularity of butterflying and dragonfly watching can be attributed, in part, to the development of standardized English names and field guides that use those names.

The group names used in this work, names such as herons and finches, are standardly used names for these groups of closely related birds. In most cases, for example loons, grebes, and hummingbirds, the group corresponds to a scientific "family." Other groups, for example geese, kites, and terns, are distinctive sub-groups within a larger family unit. In the headings in this work, when two names are connected by an ampersand, such as albatrosses & shearwaters/petrels, this means that each group is a separate family — the albatross family and the shearwater/petrel family. When two names are connected by the word "and," such as boobies and gannets, this means that they are part of the same family, in this case, the booby family.

Headings

The headings used in this section and their meanings are as follows:

NO. OF SPECIES: The number given here is the number of species regularly seen in the region that is covered by this book: the "Lower 48," that is, the lower forty-eight states of the continental United States. If two numbers are given, the numbers refer to the first and second group mentioned in the heading, respectively. For example, on pages 56 and 57, storks and ibises are treated. The number of species is given as 1 + 3. This means that there is one species of stork and three species of ibises that are regularly found in the Lower 48.

SIZE: In most cases, size is given as the distance from the tip of the bill to the tip of the tail. Occasionally, wingspan — measured from the tip of one wing to the tip of the other wing — is given. Unless explicitly stated otherwise, if there are two or more groups treated on the same two-page spread, the size range given applies to all the groups.

HOW TO KNOW THEM: This section describes how to recognize a bird as belonging to the particular group being treated. Many of the groups are composed of species that are very similar to each other but quite dissimilar in appearance from other species. For example, all hummingbirds are quite similar to each other in general appearance and no other birds really resemble them. Recognizing a species as belonging to these groups should be relatively easy. Other groups are composed of more varied species and/or are not so dissimilar in appearance from other species. Recognizing a species as belonging to these groups will be more difficult.

WHERE THEY LIVE: A very general description of the habitats in which you might find members of this group is given. During migration, many species of birds may be found in habitats that are quite different from the ones they inhabit during their breeding or wintering seasons.

WHAT THEY EAT: A short menu of the usual dietary preferences of the group is given.

SOUNDS: A general idea of the calls and/or songs of birds in this group.

ETC.: Thoughts that do not naturally fit into one of the above categories.

MAP: Shows the range of this group in the Lower 48. Most maps show the range of the group as a whole, showing where you can expect to find at least some members of this group in the summer, during migrations, and in the winter. The species present in a particular locality may not be the same in the different seasons. For example, the map for the wood warbler group shows that various species of warblers can be found on Long Island, New York all year long. In the summer, Yellow Warblers, Common Yellow-throats, and other species may be found breeding. Some Yellow-rumped Warblers spend the winter on Long Island, especially on the beaches. And, during migrations, many species can be found at this location.

In some instances the range of a particular species is given. For example, the map on page 94 shows the range of quail. The map shows where only Northern Bobwhites are found, where all other species (as a group) are found, and where both Northern Bobwhites and other quail both occur. So, if you see a quail in the range shown as having only Northern Bobwhites, it is almost certainly a Northern Bobwhite.

Above: Violet-green Swallow.

Loons   No. of species: 4

SIZE: 24 to 34 inches

HOW TO KNOW THEM: Loons are large, sleek waterbirds with sharp, dagger-like bills that distinguish them from ducks, geese, and cormorants. They ride low in the water and dive frequently for food. Their body shape is longer than that of most ducks. Loons trade their boldly patterned breeding plumage for drab, generic grays in winter, making them challenging to identify.

WHERE THEY LIVE: Northern lakes and large ponds in summer; coastal waters and larger inland lakes in winter. Adults build floating nests of reeds and other aquatic vegetation along the edges of lakes and large ponds.

WHAT THEY EAT: Small fish, crustaceans, other sea life, some plant material.

SOUNDS: The eerie yodeling wail of the male Common Loon, a defining sound of the north woods, can be heard several miles away.

ETC.: Unlike most birds, loons have marrow-filled bones that allow them to dive as deep as 250 feet. Their webbed feet are set far back on the body, making them slow and clumsy on land. Though the more northerly loon species seldom encounter people, Common Loons are vulnerable to human disturbance during nesting as well as heavy-metal poisoning from pollution and fishing weights.

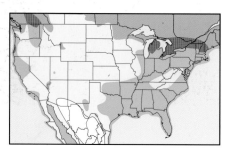

Range of loons in migration.

● Range of loons in summer.

● Range loons in winter.

◐ Range where loons are found all year.

Opposite: Common Loon. ***Above:*** Red-throated Loon.

Grebes No. of species: 7

SIZE: 10 to 25 inches

HOW TO KNOW THEM: Most species are smaller than loons, and their pointed bills help to distinguish them from ducks. Black, white, gray, and brown are the predominant plumage colors, but Eared and Horned Grebes sport tufts of golden plumes on their heads during the breeding season. Like loons and diving ducks, grebes are skillful swimmers and spend much of their time underwater.

WHERE THEY LIVE: Lakes, ponds, and marshes year round; also coastal waters in winter. Eared Grebes are found mainly on salt lakes from fall through spring. Nests are floating platforms of plant material usually anchored to aquatic vegetation, where they are vulnerable to boat traffic.

WHAT THEY EAT: Fish, amphibians, and a wide variety of invertebrates, mostly captured underwater or at the surface. Grebes also eat their own feathers, which are later regurgitated to clear the stomach of indigestible parts of their prey.

SOUNDS: A variety of cackles, hoots, and trills, mainly during the nesting season.

ETC.: The larger grebes, such as Western Grebe and Clark's Grebe, are famous for their elaborate and dramatic courtship rituals. Smaller grebes often sunbathe by turning away from the sun and lifting their wings to expose a patch of black skin.

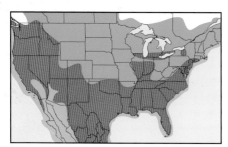

● **Range of grebes in summer.**
● **Range of grebes in winter.**
◐ **Range where grebes are found all year.**

Opposite: Red-necked Grebe with chicks. ***Top:*** Pied-billed Grebe. ***Bottom:*** Horned Grebe.

Storm-Petrels, Tropicbirds & Frigatebirds

No. of species: 8 + 3 + 1

SIZE: 7 to 40 inch length, 16 to 90 inch wingspan

HOW TO KNOW THEM: Storm-petrels are tiny, graceful seabirds related to albatrosses and shearwaters. They are so well adapted to life at sea that they are rarely seen from land. They often patter their large webbed feet on the water as they hover to pluck prey from the surface. Tropicbirds resemble large terns with white and black plumage, yellow to red bills, and central tail feathers elongated into streamers. Frigatebirds are all black or black and white with long, hooked bills, long pointed wings, and narrow, deeply forked tails.

WHERE THEY LIVE: Open oceans, islands, and coastlines. Storm-petrels nest underground in dense colonies on offshore islands, visited mostly at night. Tropicbirds and frigatebirds are mostly tropical, nesting on small islands and visiting the southern coasts of the United States.

WHAT THEY EAT: Small fish, planktonic crustaceans, squid taken from the surface.

SOUNDS: Silent except for night-time visits to nesting colonies.

ETC.: Named for a fast, maneuverable pirate ship, frigatebirds steal prey from other birds in addition to catching fish on their own. During courtship, males inflate a heart-shaped "balloon" of red skin on their throats.

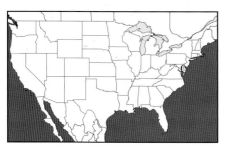

● **Range where storm-petrels and/or tropicbirds and/or frigatebirds are found.**

Opposite: Red-tailed Tropicbird. ***Top:*** Wilson's Storm-Petrel. ***Bottom:*** A male Magnificent Frigatebird displaying.

Boobies and Gannets — No. of species: 4

SIZE: 15 to 37 inch length, 37 to 72 inch wingspan

HOW TO KNOW THEM: Large, streamlined seabirds, these aerial hunters plunge like spears into schools of fish near the surface. They have long, thick necks and large pale bills that come to a sharp point. Northern Gannets and Masked Boobies are mostly white with black wings. Brown Boobies are primarily dark brown with white bellies. Young birds of all three species are dark brown or gray mottled with varying amounts of white.

WHERE THEY LIVE: Boobies live mainly in tropical oceans and are usually seen off our southern coasts. Northern Gannets are seen along the Atlantic Coast and occasionally follow schools of fish near to shore. Most species nest in colonies on inaccessible cliffs or islands.

WHAT THEY EAT: Schooling fish captured by dramatic plunging dives, sometimes from great height. When prey is sighted, the bird drops headfirst toward the surface, folding its wings back along its body before entering the water.

SOUNDS: Generally quiet away from the nesting grounds.

ETC.: Both boobies and gannets engage in elaborate courtship displays that include bowing, head-shaking, bill touching, and mutual preening. Boobies have colorful, fully webbed feet that are often used like semaphore flags during these rituals.

● **Range of gannets and boobies.**

Opposite: Blue-footed Boobies. ***Top:*** Red-footed Booby. ***Bottom:*** Brown Booby.

Pelicans No. of species: 2

SIZE: 48 to 62 inch length, 84 to 108 inch wingspan

HOW TO KNOW THEM: Up close, pelicans are unmistakable. The long, hook-tipped bills with their thin-walled pouch gives them a distinctive silhouette. Despite their ungainly appearance on land, they are graceful both on the water and in flight. Brown Pelicans are seldom confused with any other bird, but American White Pelicans resemble Snow Geese, Wood Storks, and Whooping Cranes, especially in flight.

WHERE THEY LIVE: Brown Pelicans are seabirds that nest on coastal islands, while White Pelicans nest on islands in inland lakes and winter in coastal areas. Large flocks of White Pelicans can be seen crossing the Great Plains in spring and fall migration.

WHAT THEY EAT: Mainly fish, especially small schooling species, and marine invertebrates. Brown Pelicans dive for prey, folding their wings back along the body to form a spear shape before plunging into the water. American White Pelicans feed while swimming on the surface, often in coordinated groups that give the appearance of a ballet.

SOUNDS: Mostly silent except on breeding grounds.

ETC.: Though still considered endangered in parts of North America, the Brown Pelican has made a remarkable comeback since the banning of DDT and related pesticides.

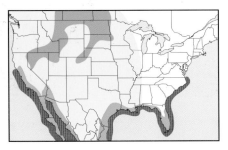

Range of pelicans in migration.

● Range of pelicans in summer.

● Range of pelicans in winter.

◉ Range where pelicans are found all year.

Opposite: American White Pelicans. **Above:** Brown Pelican.

Anhinga & Cormorants No. of species: 1 + 5

SIZE: 25 to 35 inches

HOW TO KNOW THEM: These are medium to large, dark waterbirds with long flexible necks and powerful, webbed feet. Cormorants have medium length to long hooked bills; Anhingas have long stiletto-like bills. All are powerful swimmers, spending much time underwater. Cormorants are strong fliers as well and are often seen overhead in long lines and V formations. The Anhinga's long white-tipped tail earned it the colloquial name "water turkey."

WHERE THEY LIVE: Cormorants are found in a variety of aquatic habitats from coastal bays and open ocean to freshwater marshes, rivers, and lakes. Anhingas are found in shallow wetlands, marshes, and estuaries of the southeastern states.

WHAT THEY EAT: Fish, crustaceans, other aquatic prey. Some species specialize in bottom-dwelling prey, others feed mainly on schooling fish. Population rebounds following the ban on DDT have brought Double-crested Cormorants into conflict with sport and commercial fishermen.

SOUNDS: Harsh croaks and barks.

ETC.: Unlike most water birds, the plumage of cormorants and Anhingas is not waterproof, which reduces buoyancy and improves underwater swimming performance.

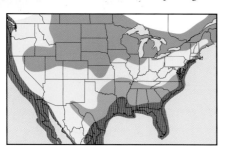

● Range of Anhinga/cormorants in migration.
● Range of Anhinga/cormorants in summer.
● Range of Anhinga/cormorants in winter.
● Range where Anhinga/cormorants are found all year.

Opposite left: An Anhinga drying its wings. Both cormorants and Anhingas spend long periods of time sunning with open wings to dry their plumage. **Opposite right:** An Anhinga takes into account the water level when making its fishing plans. **Above:** A Double-crested Cormorant with both crests ablazing.

Herons, Egrets, and Bitterns No. of species: 12

SIZE: 13 to 46 inches

HOW TO KNOW THEM: These long-legged, long-necked wading birds are a familiar sight in wetlands across North America. They range in size from the diminutive Least Bittern, a foot-tall waif of reed beds, to the stately Great Blue Heron. All have long spear-like bills and flexible necks with a distinct kink in the middle. Unlike other long-necked birds, they typically fly with their necks retracted into an "S" shape. Ibises have longer, curved bills while cranes have a bustle of feathers over their rumps.

WHERE THEY LIVE: Shallow water, both salt and fresh, across the continent; Cattle Egrets on pastureland. Herons and egrets gather in large, noisy nesting colonies called "rookeries" where they build flimsy stick nests in the tops of trees or large shrubs. Often several species will share a rookery with other colonial waterbirds such as cormorants, ibises, and spoonbills. Most are migratory, retreating to the tropics or southern coastal areas in winter.

WHAT THEY EAT: Primarily fish, but also amphibians, reptiles, crustaceans, insects. Prey is usually stalked through shallow water and captured with lightning-quick thrusts of the bill. Diversity in hunting styles is one factor that allows multiple species of herons and egrets to coexist with limited competition for food.

(*continued on page 54*)

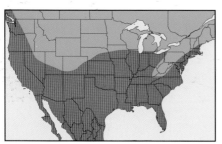

● **Range of bitterns and herons in summer.**
● **Range where bitterns and herons are found all year.**

Opposite: A white phase Reddish Egret hunts for food. ***Above:*** A Great Blue Heron with young.
Above inset: A Cattle Egret in breeding plumage.

Herons, Egrets, and Bitterns (*continued*)

WHAT THEY EAT (*continued*): Reddish Egrets shuffle their feet in shallow water to stir up prey. Green Herons have been observed using feathers and other debris to lure minnows within striking range. Cattle Egrets exploit an unoccupied ecological niche by hunting insects among the feet of livestock in meadows and pastures. Sometimes they even ride on the cattle's back!

NIGHT-HERONS: More compact and secretive than other herons, night-herons are most active between dusk and dawn. Their bills are shorter and thicker than are those of other herons, to better catch their specialized prey of crayfish and aquatic insect larvae. Two species of night-herons, the Yellow-crowned and Black-crowned, are found in the United States.

SOUNDS: Generally quiet, but croaks and grunts may be heard in nesting colonies or in alarmed flight. Night-herons make a loud "QUAK!" that is often heard after dark.

ETC.: Commercial hunters once targeted nesting colonies, killing adults for their elegant nuptial plumes and leaving nestlings to die. The National Audubon Society, founded in 1905 to put an end to the feather trade, took the Great Egret as its symbol. Cattle Egrets are newcomers to the New World, arriving in South America from Africa in the late 1800s and spreading to North America by the 1950s.

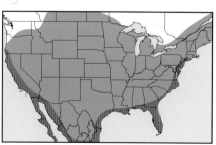

- Range of night-herons in summer.
- Range where night-herons are found all year.

Opposite: Green Heron. ***Above:*** Least Bittern. ***Above inset:*** Yellow-crowned Night-Heron.

Storks & Ibises No. of species: 1 + 3

SIZE: 23 to 52 inches

HOW TO KNOW THEM: Both storks and ibises are long-legged, long-necked wading birds with long decurved bills. The storks are large, gangly birds that might be mistaken for herons or cranes except for their huge bills and naked heads and necks. Ibises are much smaller with slimmer bills. Ibises and Wood Storks often travel in large flocks.

WHERE THEY LIVE: Marshes, shallow water of lakes and ponds, wet grasslands and prairies.

WHAT THEY EAT: Fish, crustaceans, reptiles, amphibians, small mammals, small birds. Both ibises and storks feed in shallow water by touch, sweeping open bills through murky water. When the bill touches prey, it can snap shut in a fraction of a second. Ibises also probe for invertebrates in soft mud. Storks often hunt along the edges of grass fires, snatching small animals as they flee the flames.

SOUNDS: Harsh croaks and a nasal grunting sound given in alarmed flight.

ETC.: The Scarlet Ibis, a South American species introduced or escaped into Florida, hybridizes with the native White Ibis. Once common residents of southern Florida, endangered Wood Storks now nest in smaller colonies as far north as South Carolina.

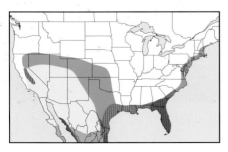

○ **Range of ibises in migration.**

● **Range of ibises in summer.**

● **Range of ibises in winter.**

◕ **Range where ibises are found all year.**

● **Range where both storks and ibises are found.**

Opposite: Wood Stork. ***Above:*** White Ibis. ***Above inset:*** Glossy Ibis.

Flamingos & Spoonbills No. of species: 1 + 1

SIZE: 32 to 46 inches

HOW TO KNOW THEM: Despite being one of the world's most recognizable birds, the American Greater Flamingo is a rare species more often seen in captivity than in the wild. Other flamingo species are kept in captivity and sometimes escape. Spoonbills, members of the ibis family, are also pink but have a long spoon-shaped bill that gives them their name.

WHERE THEY LIVE: Coastal marshes and wetlands.

WHAT THEY EAT: Flamingos specialize in tiny crustaceans that live in shallow salt water, feeding with sweeping motions and filtering the water through comb-like plates inside the bill. Spoonbills typically touch-feed in murky water like storks and ibis. The red pigments in their food give the birds' plumage its distinctive color.

SOUNDS: Usually quiet, may give nasal croak in alarmed flight.

ETC.: Roseate Spoonbills were once hunted to the edge of extinction for their beautiful feathers. Since given protection from plume hunters, they have made a comeback throughout their range. They are usually placed in the same family as ibises. Over a century ago, flocks of wild flamingos from the Bahamas regularly visited Florida Bay in what is now Everglades National Park. Most seen today are escaped birds, although some Florida and Texas birds may have come from nearby wild populations.

● **Range of Roseate Spoonbill.**
● **Range where both Roseate Spoonbill and Greater Flamingo are found.**

Opposite: Roseate Spoonbills. ***Above:*** Greater Flamingo.

Swans No. of species: 3

SIZE: 52 to 60 inch length, 66 to 80 inch wingspan

HOW TO KNOW THEM: Swans are large, graceful waterbirds that are entirely white except for feet, bill, and eyes. The bill is black except in Mute Swans, which have red bills. Snow Geese are similar in color but smaller with shorter necks, black wingtips, and pink bills.

WHERE THEY LIVE: Lakes, ponds, large rivers, marshes, coastal bays, and estuaries.

WHAT THEY EAT: Rushes, eelgrass, algae and other aquatic vegetation, aquatic invertebrates, fish eggs and fry year round, supplemented with grasses and grains in winter.

SOUNDS: Tundra and Trumpeter Swans make honking or yodeling calls similar to those of geese, while Mute Swans, despite their name, have a variety of bugles, hisses, snorts, and grunts.

ETC.: Since escaping from collections of ornamental waterfowl, the aggressive Mute Swan has done great damage to native wetlands such as the marshes of Chesapeake Bay. In contrast, populations of the native Trumpeter Swan devastated in the 1800s by unregulated hunting are still in recovery after nearly a century of legal protection and management.

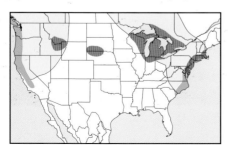

 Range of swans in migration.
 Range of swans in winter.
 Range where swans are found all year.

Opposite: Tundra Swans. **Above:** Mute Swan.

Geese   No. of species: 6

SIZE: 23 to 28 inches

HOW TO KNOW THEM: These large, gregarious waterfowl are among the most familiar of North American birds. The best known species is the Canada Goose, whose honking calls and V-shaped flight formations have come to symbolize the changing seasons. The plumage of most species is gray or brown with accents of black and white, alike in both sexes. Snow and Ross's Geese occur in two color forms, white and "blue" (actually a deep slaty gray).

WHERE THEY LIVE: Lakes, ponds, marshes, and farmlands from fall through spring. The Canada Goose is the only species that nests in the Lower 48 states; all others nest in the far north, mostly on tundra.

WHAT THEY EAT: Herbivorous. Most species eat grasses, berries, roots, and grains. The seagoing Brant specializes in sea grasses and algae.

SOUNDS: Canada Geese honk, others give a high pitched bark or yelp. All species hiss when frightened or angry.

ETC.: Canada Geese (incorrectly called "Canadian" Geese) have adapted well to development, colonizing parks, neighborhoods, and golf courses. Some populations no longer migrate, content to remain year-round in urban areas where food and protection from predators are assured.

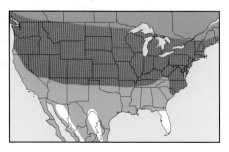

- Range of geese in summer.
- Range of geese in winter.
- Range where geese are found all year.

Opposite: Snow Geese. ***Above:*** Canada Goose. ***Above inset:*** Snow Geese.

Whistling-Ducks & Wood Ducks No. of species: 2 + 1

SIZE: 18 to 25 inches

HOW TO KNOW THEM: Whistling-ducks, once known as tree-ducks, are long legged, goose-like birds that fly with a peculiar hunchbacked posture. Their plumage, alike in both sexes, is a mix of rusty brown, black, and cream. Male Wood Ducks are among the world's most beautiful birds, with a kaleidoscope of gaudy colors and patterns; females are more subtly plumaged in browns and grays with touches of iridescence.

WHERE THEY LIVE: Whistling-ducks live in subtropical marshes and swamps in the southern United States. Wood Ducks nest primarily in swamps and river-bottom forests with other wetland habitats nearby for foraging. Black-bellied Whistling-Ducks and Wood Ducks nest in tree cavities; Fulvous Whistling-Ducks nest in marsh grasses, wet pastures, and weedy rice fields.

WHAT THEY EAT: Seeds, including cultivated grains, and aquatic vegetation are important food items for all three species. Wood Ducks also eat acorns and other nuts, wild fruits, and a higher proportion of invertebrates.

SOUNDS: All three species make high pitched whistles and squeals.

ETC.: Once endangered by overhunting and loss of habitat, Wood Ducks have rebounded thanks to hunting restrictions, habitat recovery, and the use of artificial nest boxes.

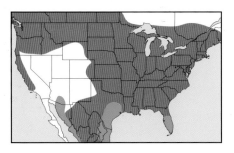

● **Range of Wood Ducks.**
● **Range where both Wood Ducks and Whistling Ducks are found.**

Opposite: A male Wood Duck. ***Top:*** Black-bellied Whistling-Duck. ***Bottom:*** Fulvous Whistling-Duck.

Dabbling Ducks   No. of species: 11

SIZE: 14 to 23 inches

HOW TO KNOW THEM: The largest group of ducks, these familiar birds feed in shallow water by dabbling at the surface or "tipping up" with their heads underwater and their tails in the air. Their bills are flattened, with a hard, claw-like nail at the tip. The Northern Shoveler gets its name from its oversized bill, which has comb-like structures to filter small crustaceans and other invertebrates from the water. Dabbling ducks ride higher in the water than many similar swimming birds. They range in size from the familiar Mallard to the tiny Green-Winged Teal. Males are usually more brightly colored than females but molt into drab "eclipse" plumage for a few weeks from late summer through early fall. Most species have a rectangular patch of iridescent or contrasting color, known as the speculum, on the trailing edge of the wing.

WHERE THEY LIVE: Widespread throughout the United States wherever there is fresh water. Most species nest from the "prairie potholes" of the northern Great Plains to the Arctic and winter southward into Mexico and the islands of the Caribbean, but many Blue-winged Teal winter in northern South America. They migrate at night.

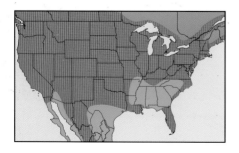

(*continued on page 68*)

- ● **Range of dabbling ducks in summer.**
- ● **Range of dabbling ducks in winter.**
- ⏺ **Range where dabbling ducks are found all year.**

Opposite: Northern Shoveler. *Above:* Male (with green heads) and female Mallards.

Dabbling Ducks (*continued*)

WHAT THEY EAT: Omnivorous, feeding on grasses, aquatic vegetation, seeds, insects, crustaceans, mussels, and snails. Farm fields, golf courses, and lawns attract flocks of grazing dabbling ducks.

SOUNDS: Females of most species quack, males give a variety of whistles, squeals, grunts, and chatters.

ETC.: Dabbling ducks are able to spring into the air from the water surface, enabling them to live on very small bodies of water. Their short legs, spaced widely, cause them to waddle when walking on land. The Mallard is arguably the most successful member of this group. Native to the northern hemisphere and widely introduced elsewhere, it is also the ancestor of most of our domestic duck breeds and still interbreeds freely with them. Unfortunately, it also interbreeds freely with its close relatives, including the Black Duck, whose populations are declining. The hybrids are fertile, and back-crossing results in genetic "swamping" of the rarer species by the Mallard. The less common Northern Pintail is another dabbling duck that is as familiar in Europe and Asia as it is in North America.

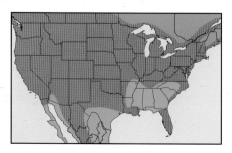

● Range of dabbling ducks in summer.
● Range of dabbling ducks in winter.
◐ Range where dabbling ducks are found all year.

Opposite: Male (foreground) and female Blue-winged Teals. **Above:** Northern Pintail. **Above inset:** Green-winged Teal.

Bay Ducks No. of species: 6

SIZE: 16 to 21 inches

HOW TO KNOW THEM: Bay ducks are stout ducks generally found on deeper waters than dabbling ducks, but sometimes with them. They are powerful swimmers, with strong legs set far back on the body, but need a running takeoff in order to take flight. Like loons and grebes, they dive frequently in search of food. Plumage coloration is much simpler than in most dabbling ducks. Males have dark heads, necks, and breasts contrasting strongly with gray to whitish sides, while females are subtle shades of brown.

WHERE THEY LIVE: Widespread. Found in a variety of aquatic habitats from freshwater lakes and rivers to coastal bays and estuaries. Many of these ducks spend the winter as part of large flocks, called rafts. The elegant Canvasback is more specialized in its nesting and feeding requirements than other bay ducks and much less common than the similar Redhead.

WHAT THEY EAT: Mussels and other mollusks, aquatic insect larvae, aquatic plants, and fish.

SOUNDS: A variety of low growls and chuckles.

ETC.: Bay ducks are strong fliers and highly migratory. Occasionally European or Asian species of ducks find their way to North America, but the sources of many unusual waterfowl species are escapees from zoos and private collections.

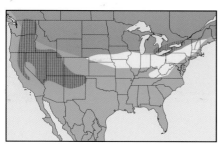

- Range of bay ducks during migration.
- Range of bay ducks in summer.
- Range of bay ducks in winter.
- Range where bay ducks are found all year.

Opposite: Redhead. ***Above:*** Ring-necked Duck. ***Above inset:*** Male and female Lesser Scaups.

Sea Ducks   No. of species: 10

SIZE: 13 to 24 inches

HOW TO KNOW THEM: Sea ducks are most often seen in winter, when flocks gravitate to southern waters. This group includes the predominantly black scoters, the colorful and bizarre eiders, the noisy Long-tailed Duck, the gaudy Harlequin Duck, and the boldly patterned goldeneyes and Bufflehead. These are hardy ducks well suited for harsh conditions. Most are stocky, compact birds with short thick necks.

WHERE THEY LIVE: Most are coastal in winter but nest on inland lakes and rivers. Scoters are often found in large flocks in ocean breakers. Harlequin Ducks nest near fast moving streams and spend winters on rocky coasts. Goldeneyes and Buffleheads nest in tree cavities near ponds or lakes and are more common on inland lakes and rivers than are their relatives.

WHAT THEY EAT: Mollusks, crustaceans, echinoderms, fish, fish eggs, algae, aquatic tubers.

SOUNDS: Mostly growls and croaks, but Long-tailed Ducks are well-known for their loud yodel. Adult male scoters and goldeneyes' wings produce a whistling sound in flight.

ETC.: The Labrador Duck, a sea duck of the northeastern Atlantic coast, was the first American bird to become extinct. The last Labrador Duck was shot in 1875.

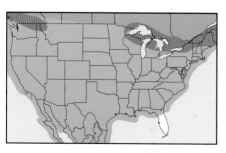

● Range of sea ducks in summer.
● Range of sea ducks in winter.
◑ Range where sea ducks are found all year.

Opposite: Bufflehead. ***Above:*** Harlequin Duck. ***Above inset:*** Surf Scoter.

Mergansers & Stifftails No. of species: 3 + 2

SIZE: 13 to 25 inches

HOW TO KNOW THEM: Mergansers are long, low-slung ducks with thin serrated bills adapted for holding prey. Both sexes have crests, an unusual feature among waterfowl. Stifftails are small ducks with chunky bodies and big heads. As the name implies, their long, stiff tails are often visible above the surface of the water. Both dive frequently and for long periods, and Ruddy Ducks often dive or swim away from danger rather than flying. Male stifftails develop a bright blue bill in the breeding season.

WHERE THEY LIVE: Both groups are widespread in a variety of aquatic habitats from ponds and rivers to coastal bays and estuaries. The distinctive Hooded Merganser, the smallest of our species and the only one restricted to North America, nests in tree cavities in swamps.

WHAT THEY EAT: Mergansers eat fish, crustaceans, and aquatic insects. Stifftails eat mostly aquatic insect larvae, other invertebrates, and plant material.

SOUNDS: Ruddy Ducks make few vocal sounds but produce a variety of mechanical drumming sounds with bill and feet in courtship displays. Mergansers are generally silent except during courtship.

ETC.: Masked Ducks, tropical stifftails, are occasionally found in south Texas.

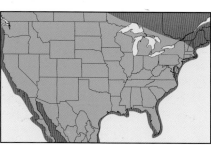

● **Range of mergansers.**
● **Range where both mergansers and stifftails are found.**

Opposite: Ruddy Duck. ***Top:*** Hooded Merganser. ***Bottom:*** Red-breasted Merganser.

Vultures   No. of species: 3

SIZE: 25 to 46 inch length, 57 to 109 inch wingspan

HOW TO KNOW THEM: Popularly known as buzzards, vultures are masters of the air, able to soar for hours with scarcely a flap of their huge wings. These large, dark birds are often seen soaring high overhead. Turkey Vultures, the most widespread species, usually soar with their wings held in a shallow "V." Their bare heads separate them from eagles and other large soaring birds.

WHERE THEY LIVE: Turkey Vultures are found throughout the United States and into southern Canada, though northern and western populations retreat southward in fall. Black Vultures are year-round residents of the southeastern and central Atlantic Coast states. After a decade in captivity, critically endangered California Condors have been returned to the mountains of southern California and the Grand Canyon in Arizona.

WHAT THEY EAT: Mostly carrion, though Black Vultures sometimes kill small prey or attack weak or sick livestock.

SOUNDS: Mostly silent, though frightened birds hiss.

ETC.: In Europe, "buzzard" is the common name of the soaring hawks also known as buteos. American vultures are more closely related to storks than to the Old World vultures, which are actually birds of prey.

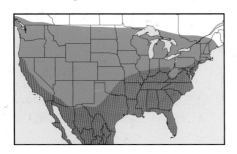

● Range of vultures in summer.
◑ Range where vultures are found all year.

Opposite left: Turkey Vulture. ***Opposite right:*** Black Vulture. ***Above:*** Black Vulture.

Ospreys & Bald Eagles No. of species: 1 + 1

SIZE: Osprey: 23 inch length, 63 inch wingspan; Bald Eagle: 26 inch length, 80 inch wingspan

HOW TO KNOW THEM: These very large raptors are predominantly blackish and white. Ospreys are boldly patterned, with a distinctive white crest and blackish mask. Bald Eagles are solid dark brown in their first plumage, becoming mottled brown and white before acquiring the pure white head and tail between five and six years of age.

WHERE THEY LIVE: Ospreys and Bald Eagles are found near both fresh and salt water, most commonly in the north and along the coasts. Nests are usually built in large trees and may be used for decades.

WHAT THEY EAT: Ospreys feed almost exclusively on fish. Bald Eagles are opportunistic, taking fish, waterfowl, mammals, and carrion. Ospreys cruise slowly over open water, often hovering briefly when a fish is spotted, then plunge feet first into the water. Bald Eagles snatch fish from the water's surface or steal them from other birds.

SOUNDS: Ospreys give a variety of shrill whistles. In movie soundtracks, the wheezy whinny of the Bald Eagle is usually overdubbed with the fiercer-sounding scream of the Red-tailed Hawk.

ETC.: Both Ospreys and Bald Eagles declined as a result of DDT and related pesticides. They have made remarkable comebacks since the 1970s but are still uncommon in many areas.

● **Range where both Ospreys and Bald Eagles are found.**

Opposite: Osprey. **Above:** Bald Eagle.

Kites & Harriers   No. of species: 5 (1 endangered) + 1

SIZE: 14 to 23 inch length, 31 to 51 inch wingspan

HOW TO KNOW THEM: Kites are a diverse group of small to medium-sized birds of prey. Some are streamlined like falcons, others short-winged like accipiters. Their habitats and food preferences are equally diverse and sometimes highly specialized. Northern Harriers are long-winged, long-tailed raptors most often spotted cruising low over open country. Adult males are dramatically different in color from females and immature males, an unusual trait in birds of prey. In all plumages, a white crescent on the rump is conspicuous, even from a distance.

WHERE THEY LIVE: Kites are found in grasslands, savannas, pastures, farmlands, marshes, swamps, wooded river corridors, and subtropical woodlands. Harriers prefer open habitats, especially marshes and grasslands.

WHAT THEY EAT: Most kites feed on small prey, especially insects, reptiles, amphibians, and small mammals, but Snail and Hook-billed kites specialize in snails. Harriers hunt extensively by ear, aided by an owl-like facial disk that concentrates sound.

SOUNDS: A variety of screams, whistles, cackles, and other calls.

ETC.: The United States population of Snail Kites, also known as Everglade Kites, is severely threatened by destruction and degradation of Florida's freshwater marshes.

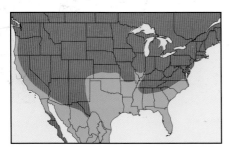

● **Range of Northern Harrier.**
● **Range where both Northern Harrier and kites are found.**

Opposite: Northern Harrier. *Above:* Mississippi Kite. *Above inset:* White-tailed Kite.

Accipiters No. of species: 3

SIZE: 10 to 26 inch length, 20 to 26 inch wingspan

HOW TO KNOW THEM: Short, rounded wings and long tails provide maximum maneuverability in tight spaces for these agile forest hawks. Adults are slaty gray to blackish above and barred with rusty brown or silver gray below. Young birds are mottled brown above, striped and barred with brown over creamy white below. The eyes start out pale amber and become orange to ruby red with age. A hawk visiting your backyard bird feeder is likely an accipiter, most likely a Sharp-shinned or Cooper's Hawk, drawn by the abundance of prey.

WHERE THEY LIVE: Forests and woodlands.

WHAT THEY EAT: Birds, small mammals, occasionally reptiles, amphibians, and invertebrates.

SOUNDS: Shrill cackles, especially around nests, kek and kip notes, other calls between mates or parents and young.

ETC.: These hawks were long reviled and persecuted, even by scientists, for their predation on songbirds, gamebirds, and the occasional barnyard fowl. Although an amendment to the federal Migratory Bird Treaty Act in 1972 banned shooting and trapping of birds of prey, accipiters are still at risk from habitat loss.

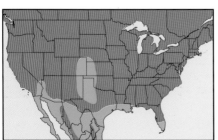

● Range of accipiters in winter.
● Range where accipiters are found all year.

Opposite: Goshawk. **Above:** Sharp-shinned Hawk.

Buteos & Golden Eagles No. of species: 13 + 1

SIZE: 15 to 30 inch length, 34 to 79 inch wingspan

HOW TO KNOW THEM: Medium to large, broad-winged hawks, the buteos are familiar North American birds of prey. They are often seen perched on utility poles or fence posts or soaring overhead. Plumage color in some species is highly variable, especially in western populations. The underparts of the common and widespread Red-tailed Hawk can be creamy white to chocolate brown. The Golden Eagle is actually a very large buteo and not closely related to the Bald Eagle.

WHERE THEY LIVE: Almost everywhere, from grasslands and farmlands to hardwood forests, swamps, and subtropical woodlands. Some buteos undertake hemisphere-spanning migrations each year while others may live their entire lives within a few miles of their birthplace.

WHAT THEY EAT: A wide variety of prey, including small to medium-sized mammals, reptiles, amphibians, crustaceans, insects, and occasionally birds.

SOUNDS: Mostly hoarse screams and mournful whistles when agitated, often around nests or in territorial interactions.

ETC.: Buteos have some of the sharpest eyes of all birds, capable of image resolution up to eight times greater than the human eye. The eyes of Golden Eagles are as large as human eyes.

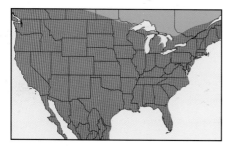

● **Range of buteos and Golden Eagles in summer.**

◐ **Range where buteos and Golden Eagles are found all year.**

Opposite: Red-tailed Hawk. ***Above:*** Swainson's Hawk. ***Above inset:*** Red-shouldered Hawk.

Falcons & Northern Caracaras   No. of species: 6 + 1

SIZE: 9 to 23 inch length, 22 to 49 inch wingspan

HOW TO KNOW THEM: Falcons are built for speed, with long, pointed wings and missile-shaped bodies. Their large eyes help them see prey from high in the air. Northern Caracara is an odd buteo-like falcon, boldly patterned in black and white with colorful facial skin and a black "toupee."

WHERE THEY LIVE: The typical falcons are found in a variety of habitats, from farm fields to arctic tundra. Many Peregrine Falcons are long-distance migrants, nesting in the far north and wintering from Mexico to Argentina. Caracaras live year round in desert scrub and subtropical woodlands of the Southwest.

WHAT THEY EAT: The larger falcons are mostly bird hunters, sometimes taking prey larger than themselves. Kestrels eat insects, small rodents, and small birds. Caracaras live more like vultures than falcons, feeding extensively on carrion in addition to reptiles, rodents, and insects.

SOUNDS: Shrill cackles and screams, especially near nests.

ETC.: Greatly admired for their skill and style in hunting, Peregrine Falcons were the most popular raptors with medieval falconers. Peregrine populations plummeted in the 1970s, but banning of DDT and related pesticides and captive breeding efforts brought this magnificent bird back to both wilderness and the skyscraper canyons of many big cities.

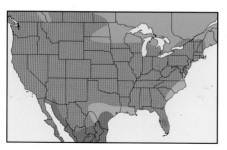

- Range of falcons in summer.
- Range of falcons in winter.
- Range where falcons are found all year.
- Range where both falcons and caracaras are found.

Opposite: American Kestrel. **Above:** Crested Caracara. **Above inset:** Prairie Falcon.

Chachalacas & Turkeys No. of species: 1 + 1

SIZE: 22 to 46 inches

HOW TO KNOW THEM: As the ancestor of one of the most familiar domestic birds and a success story in conservation, the magnificent Wild Turkey needs no introduction. The pheasant-sized Plain Chachalaca is the only member of its tropical family in the United States. Its rollicking choruses are far more attention-getting than its drab olive plumage, which is identical in both sexes. Chachalacas travel in flocks and family groups; pairs bond for life. Like most fowl-like birds, turkeys and chachalacas are weak fliers.

WHERE THEY LIVE: Wild Turkeys are found in forests and woodlands throughout the United States. They are increasingly found in suburbia as well. Plain Chachalacas are found in subtropical woodlands from southernmost Texas to Central America.

WHAT THEY EAT: Nuts and other seeds, fruits, buds, flowers, insects, and occasionally small reptiles and amphibians.

SOUNDS: The loud gobble of a tom turkey is a familiar sound; however, turkeys have an extensive vocabulary that includes clucks, yelps, whistles, cackles, and purrs. The chachalacas are named for their raucous call, often given.

ETC.: Benjamin Franklin admired the Wild Turkey and proposed it for the national symbol of the newly independent United States.

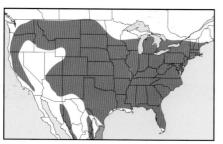

● **Range where Wild Turkeys are found all year.**
● **Range where Chachalacas are found all year.**

Opposite: Plain Chachalaca. ***Above:*** Wild Turkey.

Grouses & Ptarmigans No. of species: 8 + 1

SIZE: 12 to 28 inches

HOW TO KNOW THEM: These distant northern cousins of barnyard fowl have short rounded wings, strong legs, and cryptically patterned plumage that blends well with their environments. Tails may be squared as in the Ruffed Grouse or pointed as in the prairie-chickens, often with contrastingly colored tips on the feathers. Ptarmigans are grouse that undergo dramatic seasonal changes in plumage color, from mottled brown in summer to almost pure white in winter. Only one ptarmigan, the White-tailed, is found south of Canada.

WHERE THEY LIVE: Prairies, sagebrush, woodlands, forests, and alpine and arctic tundra.

WHAT THEY EAT: Seeds, fruits, leaves, and insects. Ptarmigans feed on nearly indigestible twigs and buds of willows and other shrubs.

SOUNDS: Mostly heard during courtship displays, when males impress prospective mates with booming, hooting, whooping, cackling, and other sounds. The Ruffed Grouse is one of several species in which non-vocal sounds produced by the wings and/or tail play a role in courtship displays.

ETC.: Prairie-chickens and the closely related Sharp-tailed and sage grouses gather each spring at traditional courting grounds known as leks, where many males simultaneously dance and display their colorful air sacs for visiting females.

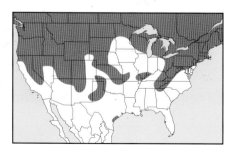

● **Range where grouse and ptarmigans are found all year.**

Opposite: A male Lesser Prairie-Chicken courting. *Above:* A Greater Sage-Grouse displays his finery to prospective mates. *Above inset:* Willow Ptarmigan.

Exotic Gamebirds No. of species: 4

SIZE: 13 to 33 inches

HOW TO KNOW THEM: These medium-sized to large ground birds are native to Europe, Asia, and Africa and were transplanted to North America to provide hunting opportunities. The Ring-necked Pheasant is a familiar sight in the Midwest and Great Plains. Both sexes have long pointed tails, but only adult males sport gaudy colors and the white collar for which the species was named. The Chukar and Gray or Hungarian Partridge, both of which have boldly striped sides, are the only widespread successes among several species of partridges released experimentally into the central and western United States.

WHERE THEY LIVE: Grasslands, hay fields, pastures, brushy areas, woodlands, and mountain slopes. Often seen near gun clubs, where pen-raised birds are released for shooting.

WHAT THEY EAT: Seeds, including cultivated grains and weed seeds, insects and other invertebrates, fruit, buds, and leaves.

SOUNDS: Clucks, cackles, chirps, hisses and whistles. Male pheasants make a crowing sound similar to that of a barnyard rooster, often accompanied by wing drumming.

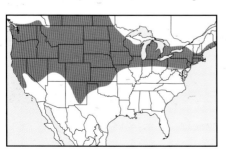

ETC.: Having lived alongside humans for much longer than their North American counterparts, pheasants and partridges often prosper in areas where agriculture has driven out native quail and grouse.

● **Range where exotic gamebirds are found all year.**

Opposite: Chukar. **Top:** Male Ring-necked Pheasant. **Bottom:** Female Ring-necked Pheasant.

Quail No. of species: 6

SIZE: 9 to 11 inches

HOW TO KNOW THEM: Quail are medium-sized, social birds that are more often heard than seen. They spend most of their time on the ground but when frightened will erupt into the air with short bursts of noisy, rapid flapping interspersed with gliding. Bold face markings often help distinguish adult males from females and youngsters. Crests help to express the bird's emotions: lowered when relaxed, raised in alarm or excitement.

WHERE THEY LIVE: Woodlands, brushy areas, desert scrub, grasslands, fallow farm fields, and hedgerows.

WHAT THEY EAT: Seeds, insects and other invertebrates, fruit, buds, and leaves.

SOUNDS: Families and coveys communicate with a complex vocabulary of chirps, cackles, whistles, purrs, and yelps. The Northern Bobwhite gets its name from the male's song, while male Gambel's and California quail seem to say, "Chi-CA-go!" Males sometimes call from the tops of large shrubs or small trees, especially in the morning.

ETC.: Once common throughout the eastern states, the Northern Bobwhite is rapidly disappearing as urban sprawl and industrial-style agriculture consume its habitat. The Masked Bobwhite, a southwestern form, almost vanished when its desert grassland habitats were overgrazed; its future is still uncertain.

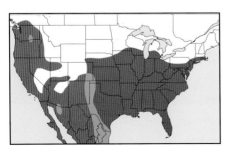

● Range where **Northern Bobwhites are found all year.**
● Range where **other quail are found all year.**
● Range where **both are found.**

Opposite: Northern Bobwhite. ***Above:*** Gambel's Quail. ***Above inset:*** Scaled Quail.

Limpkin & Rails   No. of species: 1 + 6

SIZE: Limpkin: 26 inches; Rails: 6 to 15 inches

HOW TO KNOW THEM: Rails are secretive chicken-like birds that live in dense marsh vegetation. They can swim but are usually seen stalking through reed beds or along the water's edge, where their muted colors and patterns blend with the background. Stealthy though they are, their nervous tail-flicking often gives them away. The larger Limpkin, named for its peculiar gait, is a brown ibis-like bird streaked and mottled with white.

WHERE THEY LIVE: Fresh and salt-water marshes, swamps, and the shores of lakes and ponds.

WHAT THEY EAT: Rails are omnivorous, eating a wide variety of seeds, plant material, and aquatic animal life, from insects and snails to small fish. Limpkins feed mainly on giant apple snails.

SOUNDS: Both rails and Limpkins are more often heard than seen. Rails give a variety of clicks, cackles, squeals, and whinnies. The distinctive wail of the Limpkin is usually heard at night.

ETC.: Rails are well adapted to slip through the dense vegetation of marshes. The phrase "thin as a rail" refers to their slight build.

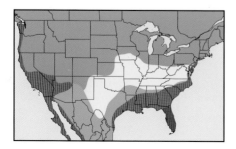

- Range of rails in migration.
- Range of rails in summer.
- Range of rails in winter.
- Range where rails are found all year.
- Range where both Limpkin and rails are found.

Opposite: Virginia Rail. *Above:* Limpkin. *Above inset:* Sora.

Coots & Gallinules No. of species: 1 + 2

SIZE: 13 to 16 inches

HOW TO KNOW THEM: These dark-plumaged relatives of the rails have chunky bodies and chicken-like bills. The American Coot is an excellent swimmer and diver, thanks to flexible flaps along the edges of its toes. Commonly called "mudhens," coots often mingle with domestic ducks around lakes and ponds in city parks. Gallinules have long legs and toes that help them scamper across soft mud and lily pads and clamber through cattails and rushes. Purple Gallinules are actually blue and green, with brilliant red and yellow bills.

WHERE THEY LIVE: Freshwater marshes, swamps, lakes, ponds, and rivers. In winter, coots may flock on protected bays.

WHAT THEY EAT: A wide variety of foods from seeds, fruits, and leaves to crustaceans, amphibians, fish, snails, and worms. Coots often graze on land, even on golf greens near water hazards.

SOUNDS: These boisterous birds make a variety of clucks, cackles, honks, and whines, especially during courtship and territorial confrontations.

ETC.: Coots often form large flocks, gallinules are less gregarious. The bird once known as the Common Gallinule is now called by its British name, Common Moorhen.

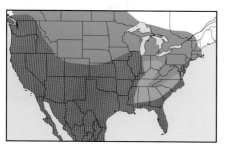

● **Range of coots and gallinules in summer.**
● **Range of coots and gallinules in winter.**
⏾ **Range where coots and gallinules are found all year.**

Opposite: Purple Gallinule. **Top.** Common Moorhen. **Bottom:** American Coot.

Cranes No. of species: 2

SIZE: 34 to 52 inch length, 73 to 90 inch wingspan

HOW TO KNOW THEM: These tall, graceful birds have bare red skin on the head and extend their long necks in flight, unlike the herons and egrets with which they are most often confused. Sandhill Cranes migrate and winter in flocks often numbering in the tens of thousands, while "Whoopers" travel in family groups of two to four individuals.

WHERE THEY LIVE: Marshes, grasslands, and arctic tundra in summer, lakes, marshes, grasslands, and farmlands in winter.

WHAT THEY EAT: Seeds, including cultivated grains, roots and tubers, insects, small mammals, amphibians, reptiles, fish, crustaceans, and mollusks.

SOUNDS: Loud bugling calls are used in courtship and territorial disputes and to keep flocks together in migration.

ETC.: Common Cranes encounter Sandhill Cranes in eastern Siberia and may follow them to wintering grounds in North America. Intensive efforts by conservationists brought Whooping Cranes back from the brink of extinction, and efforts are underway to establish new populations.

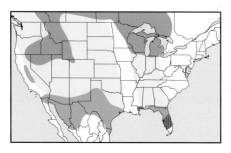

Most of North America's cranes gather at the Platte River in Nebraska during migration.

○ Range of cranes in migration.
● Range of cranes in summer.
● Range of cranes in winter.
◉ Range where cranes are found all year.

Opposite: Sandhill Crane. ***Above:*** Adult and immature Whooping Cranes.

Typical Plovers No. of species: 6

SIZE: 6 to 11 inches

HOW TO KNOW THEM: Plovers can be distinguished from other shorebirds by their shorter bills and peculiar habit of running in short spurts interspersed with abrupt stops. Most typical plovers sport black or brown rings at the base of the neck. The Killdeer is the largest of the group and the only one with double rings.

WHERE THEY LIVE: Most species inhabit beaches and mudflats. The Killdeer also uses drier locations such as lawns, golf courses, even flat gravel roofs. The drab Mountain Plover nests mainly in shortgrass prairies, often in prairie dog towns, and winters in native grasslands, close-cropped pastures, and hayfields. Nests consist of simple scrapes in the ground lined with pebbles and other debris. The fluffy chicks usually leave the nest within hours of hatching.

WHAT THEY EAT: Insects and other invertebrates.

SOUNDS: A variety of mellow to strident whistled notes. The Killdeer was named for its call.

ETC.: Killdeers are well known for their "broken-wing" distraction display, a ploy used by many birds to lure predators away from their nests or young. Tiny Piping and Snowy Plovers are threatened by recreation and resort development on their nesting beaches.

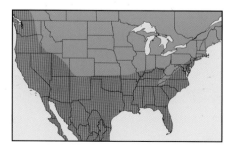

● Range of typical plovers in summer.
◑ Range where typical plovers are found all year.

Opposite: Killdeer. ***Top:*** Piping Plover. ***Bottom:*** Mountain Plover.

Golden and Black-bellied Plovers No. of species: 3

SIZE: 10 to 12 inches

HOW TO KNOW THEM: Large, sturdy plovers, these birds undergo a dramatic change from the breeding season to the winter. Adults in breeding plumage are unmistakable, with their black breasts and throats, white-sided necks and brightly variegated backs. In winter they are much duller with light, streaked breasts. Upright posture and quick foraging runs are characteristic.

WHERE THEY LIVE: Prairies, mudflats, beaches. Tundra in summer.

WHAT THEY EAT: Insects, mollusks, crustaceans.

SOUNDS: Calls in flight with high whistles.

ETC.: These long-winged birds are well adapted for long distance flight. All three species nest on Arctic tundra, placing simple nests of grasses and lichens on the ground. All undertake long migrations. Black-bellied Plovers and American Golden-Plovers migrate from the Arctic to South America (although Black-bellied Plovers also winter in the United States). Pacific Golden-Plovers summer in western Alaska (and Siberia) and winter in southern Asia and on Pacific islands, and rarely in California.

Range of golden and Black-Bellied Plovers in migration.

Range of golden and Black-bellied Plovers in winter.

Opposite: Black-bellied Plover in breeding plumage. ***Above:*** American Golden-Plover. ***Above inset:*** Winter plumaged Black-bellied Plover.

Avocets & Stilts No. of species: 1 + 1

SIZE: 14 to 18 inches

HOW TO KNOW THEM: These slim, leggy, boldly patterned shorebirds are virtually unmistakable. Both have long, thin bills, that are straight in stilts and curved upward in avocets. The Black-necked Stilt sports tuxedo-like black and white plumage accented with bubble-gum-pink legs. The American Avocet is mostly white with broad black stripes on the wings and blue-gray legs; its head, neck, and breast are whitish in winter and washed with cinnamon in the breeding season.

WHERE THEY LIVE: Shallow water in open landscapes, including permanent wetlands, seasonal ponds, tidal mudflats, and manmade evaporation ponds.

WHAT THEY EAT: Mostly invertebrates, including insects, crustaceans, small mollusks, and worms. Avocets also eat seeds; stilts occasionally feed on small fish, frogs, and tadpoles. Both species commonly peck prey from the surface of water, mud, or sand and tough-feed by "scything," sweeping the surface of the water or mud with the bill.

SOUNDS: Stilts yap, avocets give repeated kleek or wheet notes. The intensity of calling is a clue to the bird's emotional state.

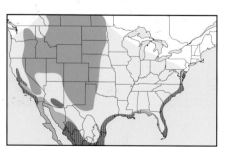

ETC.: Avocets are excellent swimmers, sometimes tipping up to feed like dabbling ducks. Stilts can swim and dive when necessary but seldom do.

- Range of avocets and stilts in migration.
- Range of avocets and stilts in summer.
- Range of avocets and stilts in winter.
- Range where both are found all year.

Opposite: American Avocet. **Above:** Black-necked Stilt.

Oystercatchers & Jacanas No. of species: 2 + 1

SIZE: Oystercatchers: 18 inches; Jacanas: 10 inches

HOW TO KNOW THEM: These large sandpiper-like birds have plumage that is extensively to entirely black. The sword-like red bills and yellow eyes of the oystercatchers create a striking contrast with their dark faces. The Northern Jacana is a tropical oddity whose extremely long toes and claws allow it to stroll lightly across floating vegetation. Both sexes have chestnut bodies, blackish heads and necks, yellow bills, yellow wing feathers, and a sharp yellow spur at the wrist joint of the wing.

WHERE THEY LIVE: The white-bellied American Oystercatcher inhabits sandy beaches and salt marshes, while the all-dark Black Oystercatcher lives among rocky tidepools and mudflats of the Pacific Coast. The Northern Jacana is common around freshwater ponds and marshes in the tropics and a rare resident of southernmost Texas.

WHAT THEY EAT: Oystercatchers feed extensively on mollusks such as oysters, mussels, and clams, stabbing their chisel-tipped bills into open shells to cut the adductor muscle that holds the halves of the shell together. Jacanas eat invertebrates and seeds.

SOUNDS: Strident piping or squealing notes.

ETC.: Female jacanas defend harems of up to four males and leave all parental care up to their mates.

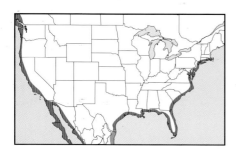

● Range of oystercatchers.
● Range where both oystercatchers and jacanas are found.

Opposite: Northern Jacana. ***Above:*** American Oystercatcher. ***Above inset:*** Black Oystercatcher.

Sandpipers No. of species: 31

SIZE: 6 to 14 inches

HOW TO KNOW THEM: One of the largest groups of birds, sandpipers are generally small, long-legged shorebirds with long, straight bills for probing sand and mud. The diversity of bill and leg lengths found in this group allows several species to forage together, each feeding in its own particular niche. A few are brightly colored, but most are drab gray or brown even in the breeding season.

WHERE THEY LIVE: Tundra, ponds, marshes, and grasslands in summer; shorelines, beaches, and tidal flats in migration and winter. Many sandpipers pass through the Lower 48 states only in spring and fall, on their way from arctic nesting grounds to winter homes in South America.

WHAT THEY EAT: Crustaceans, mollusks, insects, worms, and other invertebrates. Most shorebirds feed by probing the mud with specialized bills or simply plucking small food items from the sand or surface of the water. Phalaropes, a group of specialized sandpipers, feed by swimming with a spinning motion that stirs up food from the bottom mud.

SOUNDS: Most calls are strident peeps.

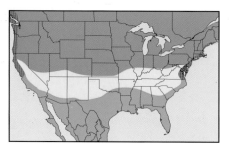

ETC.: In phalaropes, the brightly colored, aggressive females compete for the attention of drabber males, who tend the eggs and young on their own.

- Range of sandpipers in migration.
- **Range of sandpipers in summer.**
- **Range of sandpipers in winter.**
- **Range where sandpipers are found all year.**

Opposite: Red-necked Phalarope. **Above:** Spotted Sandpiper, the most widespread sandpiper in summer. **Above inset left:** Least Sandpiper. **Above inset right:** Dunlin.

Godwits & Curlews No. of species: 2 + 3 (1 endangered)

SIZE: 15.5 to 23 inches

HOW TO KNOW THEM: These oversized sandpipers can be recognized by their distinctive bills. The long, upswept bills of godwits are pink at the base and black at the tip; the equally long decurved bills of curlews (including Whimbrels) are mostly dark. Their plumage is mottled and barred in muted shades of brown, tan, cinnamon, and gray.

WHERE THEY LIVE: Prairies, arctic tundra, and farm fields in summer, prairies, marshes, ponds, tidal flats, sandy beaches, and farm fields in migration and winter.

WHAT THEY EAT: Mollusks, crustaceans, insects, worms, and tubers. Locusts and other grasshoppers are a particularly important food source in spring migration. Eskimo Curlews feed extensively on berries in fall to fatten for migration.

SOUNDS: Curlews are named for their characteristic plaintive call. Marbled Godwits also make shrill cries that resemble their name.

ETC.: In the late 19th and early 20th centuries, curlews and godwits were frequent targets for market hunters. Even after the commercial slaughter was stopped, population recovery was thwarted by loss of prairie habitats to agriculture. The smallest, the Eskimo Curlew, was virtually extinct by the 1930s, but occasional unconfirmed sightings bolster hope that a few survive.

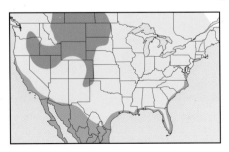

- Range of godwits and curlews in migration.
- Range of godwits and curlews in summer.
- Range of godwits and curlews in winter.

Opposite: Whimbrel. *Above:* Marbled Godwit.

Woodcocks & Snipes No. of species: 1 + 1

SIZE: 10 to 11 inches

HOW TO KNOW THEM: These short, round shorebirds with long straight bills are usually seen as they flush from underfoot. Both are cryptically colored, blending well with their habitats. Woodcocks have large eyes set high on their heads, allowing them to see danger from any direction as they forage.

WHERE THEY LIVE: Marshes, moist brushy woodlands, wet meadows, and bogs. Woodcock prefer drier habitats than snipe.

WHAT THEY EAT: Earthworms, insects, millipedes, centipedes, small amphibians and reptiles, seeds of sedges and grasses. Both species have sensitive, flexible bill tips that allow them to capture prey underground.

SOUNDS: The outer wing feathers of male woodcock are narrowed to create a whistling sound in flight. Male snipe have stiletto-like outer tail feathers that produce a shrill whinny ("winnow") during territorial flight displays. Snipe give a raspy chirp when flushed.

ETC.: The woodcock is also known among hunters as "timberdoodle" and "bog sucker." Snipe are also hunted as a game species, though this has little to do with the infamous practical joke involving a burlap bag and a remote location.

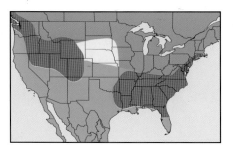

● Range of woodcock and snipe in migration.
● Range of woodcock and snipe in summer.
● Range of woodcock and snipe in winter.
● Range where woodcock and snipe are found all year.

Opposite: American Woodcock. **Above:** Wilson's Snipe.

Gulls No. of species: 20

SIZE: 11 to 30 inches

HOW TO KNOW THEM: Gulls as a group are familiar to everyone, with non-birders often referring to them as "seagulls." Most species have color patterns with combinations of gray, black, and white with black wingtips.

WHERE THEY LIVE: Gulls are a familiar sight in coastal areas but can be seen virtually anywhere in North America, especially around lakes, rivers, and reservoirs.

WHAT THEY EAT: Virtually anything, including sea life of all kinds, insects, small mammals, reptiles, amphibians, birds and their eggs, carrion, and garbage. Often harass other birds with the intent of stealing their food.

SOUNDS: These noisy birds communicate with a complex vocabulary of caws, screams, croaks, and cackles, each with a different social function. Laughing and Mew Gulls were named for their calls.

ETC.: With their opportunistic feeding habits, gulls have benefitted from human activities including commercial fishing and waste disposal. California Gulls nest at Great Salt Lake in Utah. History credits these birds with saving the crops of pioneers from an invasion of grasshoppers.

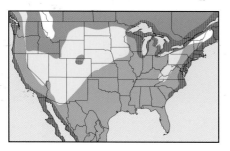

● Range of gulls in migration.
● Range of gulls in summer.
● Range of gulls in winter.
● Range where gulls are found all year.

Opposite: Laughing Gull. **Above:** Ring-billed Gull. **Above inset:** Western Gull.

Terns & Skimmers No. of species: 14 + 1

SIZE: 9 to 21 inches

HOW TO KNOW THEM: Generally smaller and slimmer than gulls, terns fly with buoyant grace. They have long pointed wings without distinct dark tips and tails that range from notched to deeply forked. Skimmers are easily recognized by their bold black and white plumage and uniquely shaped red and black bill.

WHERE THEY LIVE: Like gulls, terns are associated with the sea, but several species are found on inland lakes, rivers, ponds, and marshes. Skimmers live near shallow coastal waters and are rarely seen far from shore.

WHAT THEY EAT: Mostly fish. Terns feed on the wing by plucking prey from the surface or hovering before plunging head first into the water. Skimmers fly low over the water, slicing the surface with their blade-like lower mandible. When the bill makes contact with a fish, it snaps shut.

SOUNDS: Terns make harsh screams, squeals, and chatters. Skimmers bark or yelp.

ETC.: The longest migration of any bird is that of the Arctic Tern, which travels approximately 25,000 miles each year between its nesting grounds in the Arctic and its "winter" home in Antarctica.

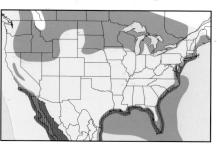

  Range of terns in migration.
● Range of terns in summer.
● Range of terns in winter.
◐ Range where terns are found all year.
● Range where both skimmers and terns are found.

Opposite: Black Skimmers feeding. ***Above:*** Royal Tern. ***Above inset:*** Black Tern.

Auks, Murres, and Puffins No. of species: 14

SIZE: 6 to 18 inches

HOW TO KNOW THEM: Also known as alcids, these odd football-shaped birds are the northern counterparts of penguins. Their stubby wings are used primarily for swimming underwater, and their flight seems labored. Most species have dark backs and white bellies that camouflage them from both predators and prey. Puffins, the best known members of this group, have colorful bill sheaths that are shed in fall and regrown each spring.

WHERE THEY LIVE: Alcids spend most of their lives at sea, coming to land only to nest. Breeding colonies are found mostly on rocky islands. An exception is the Marbled Murrelet, which nests in mossy trees in temperate rainforests of the Pacific Northwest.

WHAT THEY EAT: Small schooling fish and small crustaceans such as krill. Alcids regularly forage between 150 and 300 feet below the surface and can dive as deep as 600 feet. Feeding grounds may be 30 miles or more from nesting colonies.

SOUNDS: Typically silent at sea, alcids chatter, squeal, and groan near nests.

ETC.: Systematic slaughter of the flightless Great Auk at its nesting colonies drove it to extinction by the middle of the 19th century.

● Range of auks, murres, and puffins in winter.

● Range where auks, murres, and puffins are found all year.

Opposite: Razorbill. ***Above:*** Atlantic Puffin. ***Above inset:*** Tufted Puffin.

Pigeons and Doves   No. of species: 10

SIZE: 6 to 15 inches

HOW TO KNOW THEM: Members of this family range in size from the bluebird-sized ground-doves to the familiar feral pigeon. They are strong, fast fliers with plump bodies and small heads. Most feed on the ground, walking with mincing steps and bobbing heads. "Pigeon" usually refers to the larger members of the family, "dove" to the smaller species.

WHERE THEY LIVE: Widespread. Feral pigeons, also known as Rock Pigeons, are a familiar urban bird around the world. Mourning Doves, one of the most numerous birds in North America, are found continent-wide in a variety of habitats. Others, such as the island-hopping White-crowned Pigeon of southern Florida, are more restricted in range and habitat.

WHAT THEY EAT: Mostly seeds, nuts, and fruits, rarely insects and snails.

SOUNDS: A variety of coos and hoots. The wings of most species make a whistling or chuckling sound in flight.

ETC.: The Passenger Pigeon is the most famous case of extinction in North America. Persecution and habitat destruction exterminated a population of billions in less than one hundred years.

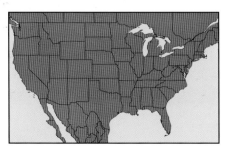

Rock Pigeons originally built their nests only on rock ledges in Europe. Now they are found around the world, nesting on human-created ledges on buildings and bridges.

● **Range where pigeons and doves are found all year.**

Opposite: Eurasian Collared Dove. **Above:** Inca Dove. **Above inset:** Rock Pigeon.

Parrots   No. of species: 2 native (1 extinct), 20+ introduced

SIZE: 6 to 18 inches

HOW TO KNOW THEM: As exotic as they seem today, flocks of colorful, noisy native parrots were once a common sight across most of the eastern and central states. In recent years, many non-native parrots have escaped from captivity, but the Monk Parakeet from South America is among the few to adapt to their new home. This long-tailed, green and gray bird is now a common resident in scattered urban areas across the country. Another success is the Red-crowned Parrot, which is considered endangered in Mexico but thrives in urban colonies in Texas, California, and Florida.

WHERE THEY LIVE: Forests, woodlands, and savannas in the tropics; greenbelts, parks, and older neighborhoods in urban areas. Most parrots nest in tree cavities, but Monk Parakeets build bulky stick nests that may be used by several breeding pairs.

WHAT THEY EAT: Fruits, seeds, nectar, other plant material.

SOUNDS: Raucous screams and squawks, shrill trills.

ETC.: Carolina Parakeet, one of two parrots native to the United States, was last reported from remote southeastern swamps in the 1930s. Thick-billed Parrots, once found in the mountains of southern Arizona, still exist in Mexico. Attempts to reestablish populations in the United States have been unsuccessful so far.

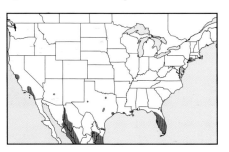

● **Range where parrots are found all year.**

Opposite: Red-crowned Parrot. ***Above:*** Green Parakeet.

Cuckoos   No. of species: 3

SIZE: 12 inches

HOW TO KNOW THEM: Slender, secretive birds of the dense forest, cuckoos are more often heard than seen. Their sleek plumage is olive above, white to cream below. They often slightly fan their long tails in flight, showing the white tips on the outer feathers. The two common species take their names from the color of their long, slightly decurved bills.

WHERE THEY LIVE: Forests, woodlands, and thickets of shrubs and young trees; Mangrove Cuckoos in mangrove swamps. Yellow-billed and Black-billed Cuckoos are long-distance migrants, wintering in South America.

WHAT THEY EAT: Mainly caterpillars, katydids, cicadas, and other large insects, occasionally small lizards and frogs. Typical hunting strategy is to sit still and scan slowly for movement. Cuckoos often gather in large numbers during outbreaks of tent caterpillars and cicadas.

SOUNDS: Hollow, liquid-sounding clucks, croaks, and coos, harsh knocking sounds.

ETC.: Many cuckoos in Europe, Africa, and Asia are brood parasites, laying their eggs in the nests of smaller birds. The Yellow-billed and Black-billed Cuckoos of North America do this occasionally but more often construct a flimsy nest and raise their own young. Many aspects of their lives are still a mystery.

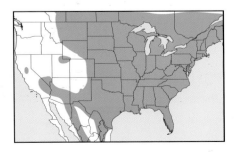

● Range of cuckoos in summer.

◗ Range where cuckoos are found all year.

Opposite: Yellow-billed Cuckoo. **Above:** Mangrove Cuckoo.

Roadrunners & Anis No. of species: 1 + 2

SIZE: 13 to 23 inches

HOW TO KNOW THEM: Roadrunners are familiar to anyone who watched Saturday morning cartoons. The Greater Roadrunner is a ground-dwelling cuckoo that can fly but prefers to run. The long tail seems to move independently of the rest of the body, rising as the bird stops. Anis resemble disheveled blackbirds with large, puffin-like bills.

WHERE THEY LIVE: Roadrunners are the quintessential desert bird but are also found in a variety of open habitats throughout their range. Anis nest in dense thickets and often forage in grassy fields, snatching insects stirred up by grazing cattle.

WHAT THEY EAT: More than half of a roadrunner's diet is invertebrates such as grasshoppers, beetles, and scorpions, but they also feed on small mammals, reptiles, birds, fruits, and seeds. Anis are primarily insectivorous, feeding on grasshoppers, cockroaches, beetles, spiders, and ticks.

SOUNDS: In contrast to its cartoon counterpart, the Greater Roadrunner coos, barks, growls, whines, and rattles its bill. The anis were named for the whiny, upslurred call of the Smooth-billed Ani.

ETC.: Roadrunners are intelligent, agile predators that could be the model for the velociraptors of Jurassic Park.

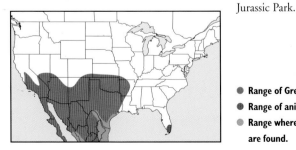

- ● **Range of Greater Roadrunner.**
- ● **Range of anis.**
- ● **Range where both Greater Roadrunner and anis are found.**

Opposite: Groove-billed Ani. ***Above:*** Greater Roadrunner.

Owls No. of species: 18

SIZE: 5 to 27 inches length, 13 to 52 inches wingspan

HOW TO KNOW THEM: Owls are a diverse group ranging from the sparrow-sized Elf Owl to the majestic Great Gray Owl. They all have large, forward-facing eyes and soft, sound-muffling plumage. Most are nocturnal and hunt using keen hearing and night vision. Their plumage typically blends well with their preferred habitat, from the arctic white of Snowy Owls to the sandy browns of Burrowing Owls.

WHERE THEY LIVE: Virtually all terrestrial habitats, from grasslands and deserts to ancient forests and arctic tundra.

WHAT THEY EAT: Live prey, from moths and crickets to snowshoe hares. Prey selection varies by owl species, habitat, and season. Owls swallow their prey whole and regurgitate the indigestible portions in compact "pellets." Dissection of these pellets reveal bones, hair, and feathers that can be used to analyze their diet.

SOUNDS: Most large owls hoot, but smaller species trill, whinny, scream, moan, and hiss. Frightened owls often snap their bills like castanets.

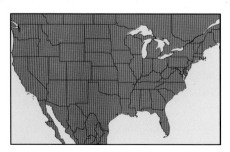

ETC.: Owls look huge, but it's mostly feathers. The soft, fluffy plumage helps to muffle sounds as the bird flies in search of prey.

(*continued on page 132*)

● **Range where owls are found all year.**

Opposite: Western Screech-Owl. ***Above:*** Great-Horned Owl.

Owls (*continued*)

GREAT HORNED OWL: The most familiar owl in North America has large yellow eyes and a scowling expression. Tufts of feathers form "horns" that add to this formidable appearance. The plumage is finely barred, streaked, and mottled — perfect camouflage against tree bark. Like other owls, Great Horned Owls do not make their own nests; instead, they take over the nests of hawks or ravens, or lay their eggs in a tree hollow, cave, or building. Lacking a sense of smell, Great Horned Owls are among the few predators that regularly take skunks.

SCREECH-OWLS: Screech-owls are smallish owls with vertically streaked undersides. Their small ear-tufts are often held flattened, giving them a round-headed appearance. Calls are eerie trilling whinnies that often arouse fear and suspicion when heard.

BARN OWL: The most widespread of all the world's owls has a unique heart-shaped facial disc that channels sound to its asymmetrical ears, allowing for very precise location of prey by sound alone. It is different enough from other owls that it is usually placed in its own family. Also called "monkey-faced owl," these birds often nest in seldom-used or abandoned buildings. Their silent flight and spine-tingling screams are responsible for many tales of haunted houses.

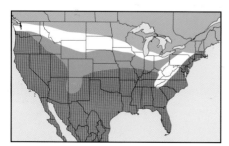

● **Range of Barn Owl in summer.**

◑ **Range where Barn Owls are found all year.**

● **Range of Snowy Owls in winter.**

Opposite: Snowy Owl. ***Above:*** Barn Owl.

Nightjars & Nighthawks No. of species: 5 + 3

SIZE: 7 to 12 inches

HOW TO KNOW THEM: Odd, big-headed night birds, members of the nightjar family have huge mouths that they use to catch moths and other night-flying insects. They are so perfectly camouflaged as to be virtually invisible as they roost on the ground or parallel to a branch. Their enormous dark eyes and soft plumage are similar to that of many owls. The owl-like nightjars are solitary and secretive. The falcon-shaped nighthawks are more gregarious, often gathering under street lamps and stadium lights to catch moths.

WHERE THEY LIVE: Forests, grasslands, deserts, mountains, and cities.

WHAT THEY EAT: Nocturnal flying insects. The largest of the nightjars sometimes eat small songbirds as they migrate at night.

SOUNDS: The nightjars take their names from the males' songs: Whip-poor-will, Chuck-will's-widow, poorwill, and Pauraque. Nighthawks, the more diurnal members of the family, make nasal or purring sounds in flight.

ETC.: Nightjars are also called "goatsuckers," a literal translation of the family name Caprimulgidae that refers to an old misconception that they used their huge mouths to suckle goats. Most nightjars migrate to avoid cold weather, but the Common Poorwill can "hibernate" for short periods in winter.

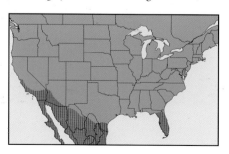

● **Range of nightjars and nighthawks in summer.**
◑ **Range where nightjars and nighthawks are found all year.**

Opposite: Common Poorwill. **Top:** Buff-collared Nightjar. **Bottom:** Chuck-will's-widow. **Bottom inset:** Common Nighthawk.

Swifts No. of species: 4

SIZE: 5 to 7 inches

HOW TO KNOW THEM: Swifts are adept aerialists, feeding, mating, and even sleeping on the wing. They are often seen overhead in erratic fluttering flight. Cigar-shaped bodies and long scythe-like wings allow for speed and quick maneuvering as they pursue flying insects. Their tiny feet are too weak for normal upright perching, so they hang vertically from rock faces and the walls of chimneys and tree hollows.

WHERE THEY LIVE: Swifts are widespread, in all habitats, throughout the Lower 48 states. All species attach their nests to vertical surfaces with saliva. As their name implies, Chimney Swifts nest mostly in chimneys. Their western counterparts, Vaux's Swifts, prefer hollow trees, making them vulnerable to forest thinning.

WHAT THEY EAT: "Aerial plankton" consisting of flying insects and young spiders adrift on silk "balloons." Even when flying through clouds of insects, their agility helps swifts target the choicest prey and avoid stinging insects.

SOUNDS: Twittering chips.

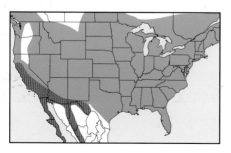

ETC.: In preparation for migration, swifts often gather by the thousands to roost in chimneys and hollow trees. Chimney Swifts migrate from the eastern United States to Amazonia each winter.

● **Range of swifts in summer.**
⬤ **Range where swifts are found all year.**

Opposite: Chimney Swift. **Above.** White-throated Swift.

Hummingbirds No. of species: 17

SIZE: 3 to 5 inches

HOW TO KNOW THEM: Hummingbirds have a unique figure-eight wing motion that allows them to hover in still air and fly in any direction, feats unmatched by any other bird. Their brilliant iridescent colors appear to wink on and off and change hue with the angle and quality of light. Adult males of most species have brighter and more extensive iridescent colors and more distinctive tail feathers than females and immature males. Many are small enough to be easily confused with large insects, but male Magnificent and Blue-throated Hummingbirds of the Southwest are almost chickadee-sized, three times the weight of a male Ruby-throated.

WHERE THEY LIVE: A variety of habitats from deserts to cool northern forests. Most species are found mainly in the West, while the Ruby-throated Hummingbird is the sole breeding species in the East. Hummingbirds are primarily tropical birds, and within the United States the greatest diversity is found along the Mexican border. Most leave the United States for the tropics in fall, but Anna's and Costa's Hummingbirds are year-round residents in the Southwest and along the Pacific Coast. In the Southeast, departing Ruby-throateds are replaced each fall by small numbers of western hummingbirds such as Rufous and Calliope.

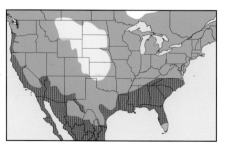

(*continued on page 140*)

- ○ Range of hummingbirds in migration.
- ● Range of hummingbirds in summer.
- ◐ Range of hummingbirds in winter.
- ⦿ Range where hummingbirds are found all year.

Opposite: Male Calliope Hummingbird. ***Above:*** Allen's Hummingbird. ***Above inset:*** Female Calliope Hummingbird.

Hummingbirds (*continued*)

WHAT THEY EAT: Long, thin bills and the ability to hover allow them to feed at nectar-rich flowers, where their tongues, tubular at the end, function like drinking straws. They also eat insects, spiders, tree sap, and sugar water from feeders. Hummingbird-pollinated flowers are often red, a color that catches the birds' attention but is largely ignored by bees.

SOUNDS: Hummingbirds can be very noisy, giving a variety of chip-notes while foraging and harsh chatters in combat. Male hummingbirds of most species are accomplished singers, even learning phrases from other hummingbirds. In a few species such as Broad-tailed, Rufous, and Black-chinned, males have modified wing feathers that create distinctive sounds in flight.

ETC.: Some species have spectacular courtship displays. A male Anna's Hummingbird will climb high into the sky and then dive straight down at tremendous speed toward a waiting female, spreading his tail feathers to produce a sound that he hopes is attractive. Feeding stations and flower-filled meadows in the western mountains are among the best places to see these living jewels, as is the Gulf Coast of Texas, where Ruby-throated Hummingbirds gather by the thousands in September.

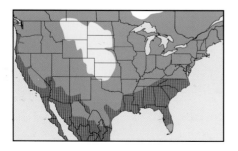

Range of hummingbirds in migration.
Range of hummingbirds in summer.
Range of hummingbirds in winter.
Range where hummingbirds are found all year.

Opposite: Female Anna's Hummingbird on her nest. *Above:* Buff-bellied Hummingbird. *Above inset:* Costa's Hummingbird.

Trogons No. of species: 2

SIZE: 12 to 14 inches

HOW TO KNOW THEM: Jay-sized birds of tropical forests, trogons reach their northern limits in the mountains along the Mexican border. Adult male Elegant Trogons and both sexes of the Eared Quetzal are brilliantly plumaged in iridescent green and rose red, while female and immature male Elegant Trogons wear muted mauves, coppery browns, and pinks. Their long tails are mostly white below and iridescent green, blue, bronze, or copper above. Loud, persistent calls often betray the presence of these otherwise secretive birds. Flight is undulating, like that of woodpeckers.

WHERE THEY LIVE: Mountains forests of oaks, pines, and firs; especially along canyon streams with sycamores and other deciduous trees. Elegant Trogons also live in a variety of other forest types in the tropics.

WHAT THEY EAT: Insects such as cicadas and caterpillars, small lizards and frogs, small fruits.

SOUNDS: Elegant Trogons sound like large frogs or distant barking dogs: "kwa-kwa-kwa-kwa." Eared Quetzals make shrill squeals and raucous cackles when disturbed; males defend territories and attract mates with a rising tremolo whistle.

ETC.: Despite being much more common in Mexico, trogons lure thousands of visitors each year to the mountains of southeastern Arizona.

● **Range of trogons in summer.**
◐ **Range where trogons are found all year.**

Opposite: Female Elegant Trogon in nesting hole. **Above:** Male Elegant Trogon.

Kingfishers No. of species: 3

SIZE: 9 to 16 inches

HOW TO KNOW THEM: These short-legged, spear-billed birds haunt the edges of rivers, streams, lakes, and ponds. Their oversized heads sport crests, spiky in the large Belted and Ringed Kingfishers, sleek in the tiny Green Kingfisher. Plumage color is basically slaty bluish or satiny green, with a broad white collar and fine white barring in the wings and tail.

WHERE THEY LIVE: Streams, rivers, lakes, and ponds. Adults excavate nest burrows in steep earthen banks.

WHAT THEY EAT: Fish and aquatic invertebrates captured by diving headfirst from perches overlooking the water. Kingfishers can also hover briefly and use this technique to spot prey in open water. Green Kingfishers occasionally hunt insects over dry land when streams are too muddy to spot fish.

SOUNDS: The rattling, machine-gun calls of kingfishers are more often heard than the birds are seen. The pitch of the call is a good indication of the size of the bird.

ETC.: Rusty red color on the underparts is found in both sexes of the Ringed but only in the female Belted and the male Green Kingfisher.

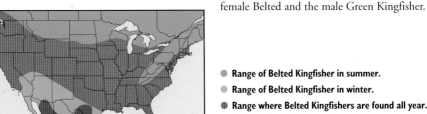

- Range of Belted Kingfisher in summer.
- Range of Belted Kingfisher in winter.
- Range where Belted Kingfishers are found all year.
- Range where Belted Kingfishers and other kingfishers are found.

Opposite: Green Kingfisher. **Above:** Belted Kingfisher eating a fish.

Woodpeckers   No. of species: 23

SIZE: 7 to 17 inches

HOW TO KNOW THEM: Woodpeckers are generally seen on tree trunks, with their heads up. Although the two species of flickers will sometimes search for insects on the ground, woodpeckers are uniquely adapted for a lifestyle of foraging for insects beneath the bark of trees. All species, from the sparrow-sized Downy to the crow-sized Pileated (see page 11), have feet adapted for gripping vertical tree trunks, stiff tails for bracing against bark, and sturdy straight bills. In most species the plumage is predominantly black and white with red or yellow accents. Woodpeckers have a characteristic undulating flight, dropping slightly between short bursts of flapping.

WHERE THEY LIVE: Any place with trees, from desert woodlands to old-growth forest. Some are adaptable enough to live in city parks and older neighborhoods, while others need certain types of wild habitat to survive. In general, woodpeckers are less migratory than many of our other birds.

WHAT THEY EAT: Grubs and other insects extracted from beneath bark using the long barbed tongue; fruit, and seeds. Some species also "hawk" flying insects. Acorn Woodpeckers store acorns in "granary trees" for future meals. Woodpeckers will feed on suet from backyard feeders.

(*continued on page 148*)

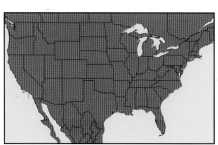

● **Range where woodpeckers are found all year.**

Opposite left: Northern Flicker. ***Opposite right:*** Red-bellied Woodpecker. ***Above:*** Downy Woodpecker.
Above inset: White-headed Woodpecker.

Woodpeckers (*continued*)

SOUNDS: Simple sharp yelps or repetitive rattling calls. Both sexes drum on hollow trees to advertise territory.

SAPSUCKERS: These unusual woodpeckers harvest the sugar-rich sap of trees through holes they drill in the living layers of the bark. The sap wells are also used by other wildlife, including hummingbirds, warblers, chipmunks, and other woodpeckers. Sapsuckers also eat bark, buds, fruit, and seeds. For protein and other vital nutrients, sapsucker eat insects, which may be gleaned from foliage, excavated from under bark, or simply plucked out of the sap wells. Parent sapsuckers often dip captured insects into sap wells before feeding them to nestlings. Current convention divides the various populations into four species.

ETC.: Woodpeckers have amazingly long tongues. When not being used to probe crevices in tree limbs, the tongue is coiled in the skull.

Woodpeckers typically excavate a new nest cavity every year. Since many other birds nest in cavities but are unable to excavate their own, woodpeckers and their abandoned nests are a crucial part of the woodland ecology. Though most woodpeckers live in "nuclear families" consisting of an adult pair and their young, Acorn Woodpeckers often live in groups that lay eggs in the same nest and cooperate in raising the young.

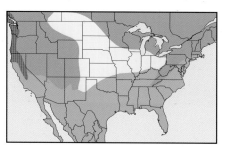

● **Range of sapsuckers in migration.**
● **Range of sapsuckers in summer.**
● **Range of sapsuckers in winter.**
● **Range where sapsuckers are found all year.**

Opposite: Acorn Woodpecker with its stash of acorns. **Opposite inset:** Red-headed Woodpecker. **Above:** Yellow-bellied Sapsucker.

Tyrant Flycatchers No. of species: 35

SIZE: 5 to 10 inches

HOW TO KNOW THEM: Flycatchers are a large and varied group that share some aspects of shape and lifestyle but little else. Most have broad, strong bills fringed in sensitive "whiskers" (rictal bristles) and an upright posture. They all feed predominantly on insects, usually captured in flight. Perhaps the best way to recognize a bird as a flycatcher is by its behavior. Typical hunting behavior of these birds is to sit quietly on an open perch, flying out periodically to snatch passing insects before returning to its original perch. Even the drab species are graceful in these feeding flights. Some, such as lipstick-red Vermilion Flycatchers and flamboyant Great Kiskadees, are hard to miss. Others are dull in color and retiring in habits, making identification difficult. For the drab species, voice and behavior are often the best clues to species. About fifteen species resemble the Willow Flycatcher shown above.

WHERE THEY LIVE: Any habitat with flying insects will have attendant flycatchers.

WHAT THEY EAT: Flying insects and small fruits. Kiskadees will also eat small fish.

SOUNDS: A variety of whistles, chatters, squeals, and chips. Flycatchers are rarely musical but their call notes can be important clues to identification.

(*continued on page 152*)

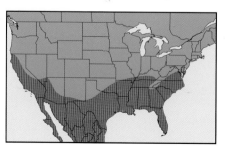

● **Range of flycatchers in summer.**

◑ **Range where flycatchers are found all year.**

Opposite: Willow Flycatcher. **Opposite inset:** Scissor-tailed Flycatcher. **Above:** Vermillion Flycatcher.

Tyrant Flycatchers (*continued*)

ETC.: Among the largest of our native flycatchers are the kingbirds, Great-crested Flycatcher and its relatives, and the Great Kiskadee. Kingbirds are famous for the fearless and pugnacious attitude that inspired both their common name and that of their family. They scan for trespassers from treetops or fenceposts in grasslands and open woodlands, attacking interlopers as large as hawks. These highly vocal birds begin the day with a special "dawn song" and can be heard calling off and on throughout the day. Long pointed wings make them particularly swift and agile fliers. Most kingbirds have gray or blackish backs, predominantly yellow or white underparts, and moderately long, squared to slightly notched tails. The Scissor-tailed Flycatcher, once known as the "prairie bird of paradise," is a kind of kingbird with an extravagant tail and sunset pink sides.

Great Crested Flycatchers in the East, and their closely related look-alikes, Ash-throated, Brown-crested and Dusky-capped Flycatchers in the West, range from 8 to 9 inches. Unlike most of our other flycatchers, all of these nest in tree cavities.

Great Kiskadees are normally resident only in south Texas, where their loud call, "Kis-ka-dee," is a characteristic sound along watercourses.

● **Range of kingbirds in summer.**
◍ **Range where kingbirds are found all year.**

Opposite: Great-crested Flycatcher. ***Above:*** Eastern Kingbird. ***Above inset:*** Great Kiskadee.

Shrikes No. of species: 2

SIZE: 9 to 10 inches

HOW TO KNOW THEM: These medium-sized pale gray birds have bold black and white wings and tails and a black mask. Though technically songbirds, shrikes behave more like tiny birds of prey. Their bills are long and hooked for tearing through skin, scales, and insect exoskeletons. Shrikes fly with rapid wing beats in direct flight and hunt by sitting on perches in the open, dashing out intermittently to chase down prey.

WHERE THEY LIVE: Grasslands with scattered shrubs, farm fields, pastures, hedgerows, deserts, and wetland edges.

WHAT THEY EAT: Almost any small animal, including insects, reptiles, small mammals, birds, even crabs in coastal areas. When food is plentiful, they cache excess prey by impaling it on thorns and barbed wire, a habit that earned them the nickname "butcherbird."

SOUNDS: Both sexes have pleasant warbling songs and shrill screeches more befitting a fierce predator.

ETC.: Loggerhead Shrikes have almost disappeared from much of the eastern United States and are declining in the Great Plains. The reasons for this are poorly understood but appear to involve both pesticides and loss of habitat to development.

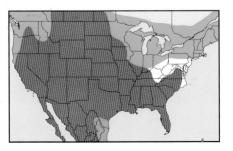

- Range of shrikes in migration.
- Range of shrikes in winter.
- Range where shrikes are found all year.

Opposite: Loggerhead Shrike. **Above:** Loggerhead Shrike.

Vireos No. of species: 14

SIZE: 5 to 6 inches

HOW TO KNOW THEM: The loud and distinctive voices of vireos make them easy to locate, but actually seeing these small, nondescript birds is another matter. They are secretive, spending most of their time in dense foliage where their muted gray to yellowish green plumage serves as excellent camouflage. Kinglets and other birds that are similar in size and color are usually detected as they hop and flutter energetically among the branches. Vireos are more deliberate, moving methodically through the tree canopy gleaning insects from leaves and bark and pausing often to look and listen for prey. Once in view, their large heads, blunt bills, and distinctive face markings help to identify them.

WHERE THEY LIVE: Forests and woodlands, often in shrub thickets or the canopy of broad-leafed trees.

WHAT THEY EAT: In summer, caterpillars and other invertebrates gleaned from crevices in bark of trees. In winter, insects and small fruits.

SOUNDS: The persistent songs of vireos often have a harsh quality and can be monotonous. The birds are so confident in their camouflage that some are even known to sing while incubating eggs.

ETC.: The Black-capped Vireo of Texas and Oklahoma is endangered.

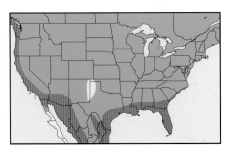

- Range of vireos in migration.
- Range of vireos in summer.
- Range where vireos are found all year.

Opposite: Blue-headed Vireo. ***Top:*** Bell's Vireo. Bottom: Red-eyed Vireo.

Jays & Nutcrackers

No. of species: 10 + 1

SIZE: 10 to 19 inches

HOW TO KNOW THEM: Jays are large, boisterous songbirds easily observed from wilderness areas to backyard bird feeders. Though most species are predominantly blue, jays also come in gray, green, and brown. Only the familiar Blue Jays of the eastern forests and Steller's Jays of the western mountains have crests. Clark's Nutcrackers are crow-like gray birds with black and white wings and tails and strong black bills that they use to hammer open seeds.

WHERE THEY LIVE: Jays are found in forests, woodlands, and city parks. Clark's Nutcrackers inhabit tall conifer forests of the Rocky Mountains and Pacific Northwest.

WHAT THEY EAT: Jays will eat almost anything but prefer insects and large seeds. Given the opportunity, they will raid the nests of other birds. Pinyon Jays specialize in the seeds of pinyon pines. Clark's Nutcracker specializes in pine seeds but also feeds on small animals and carrion.

SOUNDS: These birds are loud and vocal but not musical. Most calls are loud harsh squawks. Most jays are talented mimics and can imitate other birds.

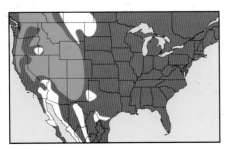

ETC.: Jays (and crows, which are in the same family as jays) will often "mob" predators. Birders often locate hawks and owls by following the loud raucous calls of jays.

● Range where jays are found all year.
● Range where both jays and Clark's Nutcracker are found all year.

Opposite left: Clark's Nutcracker. ***Opposite right:*** Green Jay. Above: Blue Jay.

Crows and Ravens & Magpies No. of species: 6 + 2

SIZE: 16 to 24 inches

HOW TO KNOW THEM: Large, raucous, gregarious, and widespread, crows and ravens are among the most recognizable of birds. All of our species are completely black. Magpies are elegant birds with boldly patterned black and white plumage. Their long tails and white-patched wings are washed with blue to bronze iridescence. Black-billed Magpies have black bills. You can guess at the color of Yellow-billed Magpies' bills.

WHERE THEY LIVE: Crows and ravens are found in all terrestrial habitats, from deserts to high mountains. Ravens are better adapted to extremely dry or cold climates. These birds also adapt well to development. Magpies need trees and shrubs for nesting and roosting but forage in a wide variety of habitats.

WHAT THEY EAT: Crows and ravens are omnivorous, feeding on almost anything, including the eggs and young of other birds. Magpies also eat almost anything but prefer insects and large seeds.

SOUNDS: A variety of caws, croaks, and rattles. Like jays, these birds are good mimics.

ETC.: Native American cultures admired crows and ravens for their intelligence and mischievous nature, though today these same qualities often lead them into conflicts with people.

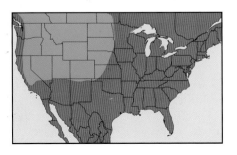

● Range where crows and ravens are found all year.
● Range where crows and ravens and magpies are found all year.

Opposite: Black-billed Magpie. ***Above:*** Common Raven. ***Above inset:*** American Crow.

Larks No. of species: 1

SIZE: 7 inches

HOW TO KNOW THEM: Although other birds share the name, the Horned Lark is the only true lark native to North America. Its "horns" are tiny curving tufts of feathers that are sometimes difficult to see. Though all members of the species have at least a suggestion of the adult male's black mask and breast band, the back color varies from dull grayish brown to warm rusty to match the local soil color. Large flocks stroll along the ground searching for seeds and insects. In flight, flocks seem to flow low over the ground like waves, accompanied by weak, lisping call notes.

WHERE THEY LIVE: Open country, including shortgrass prairies, deserts, pastures, and agricultural fields. The nest is a cup of fine plant material in a shallow depression in bare ground.

WHAT THEY EAT: Insects and seeds.

SOUNDS: Flocks communicate with see-tee or see-tiu notes. Males sing a bright, breezy jumble of metallic notes in flight, a behavior common among larks.

ETC.: Singing in flight, a behavior known as "skylarking," is not unique to the larks. The Lark Sparrow and Lark Bunting are sparrows that were named for this habit.

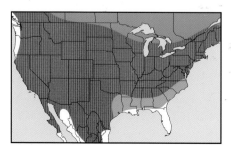

● **Range of Horned Larks in summer.**
● **Range of Horned Larks in winter.**
◐ **Range of where Horned Larks are found all year.**

Opposite: Female Horned Lark with young. **Above:** Male Horned Lark.

Swallows No. of species: 8

SIZE: 5 to 8 inches

HOW TO KNOW THEM: Among the most familiar of all birds, swallows are master aerialists, capable of drinking and even bathing on the wing. Their acrobatic flight and long, pointed wings help to distinguish them from other songbirds. Though similar in size, shape, and lifestyle to the swifts, their wingbeats are more fluid and graceful. Tiny bills open to reveal a wide mouth adapted for snatching insects out of the air. Short legs and dainty feet are almost useless for walking.

WHERE THEY LIVE: Almost anywhere flying insects are found, including open fields, lakes, marshes, forests, grasslands, and deserts. Nesting often takes place in large colonies. Nests are usually made from mud and plant fibers attached to a rock face or building or placed inside a tree cavity or burrow. Migrating swallows often gather by the thousands to roost in trees, marsh vegetation, or crops such as sugarcane.

WHAT THEY EAT: Primarily insects and spiders, though Tree Swallows feed extensively on bayberries in fall and winter.

SOUNDS: A variety of twittering and chattering calls.

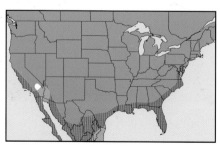

ETC.: Despite claims to the contrary, there is little evidence that Purple Martins, a kind of swallow, regularly feed on mosquitoes.

● **Range of swallows in summer.**
● **Range of swallows in winter.**
◗ **Range where swallows are found all year.**

Opposite: Barn Swallow. Above: Tree Swallow. **Above inset:** Cliff Swallow.

Titmice No. of species: 5

SIZE: 5 to 7 inches

HOW TO KNOW THEM: These small, inquisitive birds have jaunty crests, short bills, and strong legs. All are predominantly gray, with markings ranging from the slightly paler bellies of Oak and Juniper Titmice to the bold harlequin head pattern of Bridled Titmice. They often hang upside down to peck at clusters of fruit, seeds, or dead leaves.

WHERE THEY LIVE: Forests and woodlands. Nests are made inside cavities in trees, usually abandoned woodpecker holes. Titmice are essentially nonmigratory, though in winter they may move short distances to find food.

WHAT THEY EAT: Insects, especially caterpillars, spiders, snails, seeds, and fruit. Titmice are frequent visitors to bird feeders. They often cache sunflower seeds and other large offerings in nearby trees for later consumption.

SOUNDS: Titmice have extensive vocabularies that include chickadee-like calls, thin, nasal whistles, and harsh scolding notes. Songs are variations on "peter-peter-peter."

ETC.: From fall through spring, titmice often flock with chickadees, bushtits, and other small birds. Despite their small size, titmice are often instigators of mobbing behavior against potential predators such as owls, hawks, cats, and snakes.

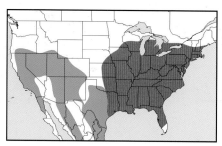

● **Range where Tufted Titmice are found all year.**
● **Range where other titmice are found all year.**

Opposite: Bridled Titmouse. ***Above:*** Tufted Titmouse.

Chickadees & Bushtit No. of species: 6 + 1

SIZE: 4 to 6 inches

HOW TO KNOW THEM: Chickadees are somewhat more familiar than their close relatives, the tit-mice. These plump, boldly marked birds with fearless, curious personalities have endeared them-selves to bird lovers throughout North America. The drab gray Bushtit is one of the smallest songbirds in North America, only slightly larger than the smaller hummingbirds. Bushtits are highly social, living year round in flocks of ten to more than forty individuals. Despite superficial similarities, this species is only a distant relative of chickadees and titmice.

WHERE THEY LIVE: Chickadees live in forests and woodlands, where they nest in tree cavities. Bushtits are found in a wider range of habitats, including thorny desert thickets. They build a hanging nest of spider silk and plant material.

WHAT THEY EAT: Insects, including caterpillars, aphids, and scale insects, spiders, fruits, and seeds. Bushtits also eat scale insects, prey too small for many other birds to bother with. Like titmice, chickadees and bushtits often hang upside down when foraging.

SOUNDS: Chickadees are among many birds named for their characteristic call, but they have complex vocabularies similar to those of the titmice. Bushtits make simple chip-notes.

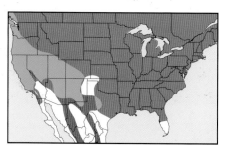

- Range where chickadees are found all year.
- Range where bushtits are found all year.
- Range where both chickadees and bushtits are found all year.

Opposite: Bushtit. ***Above:*** Black-capped Chickadee.

Verdin & Creepers No. of species: 1 + 1

SIZE: 4 to 5 inches

HOW TO KNOW THEM: Tiny, yellow-faced Verdins are sprightly desert dwellers. Though active and vocal, their small size can make them hard to spot. These distant cousins of chickadees and titmice often hang upside down while searching for food. The Brown Creeper is a songbird that behaves like a tiny woodpecker, clinging to the trunks and limbs of trees as it probes bark crevices with its long, thin bill. Its plumage is streaked to mimic fissured bark. Creepers move up the trunks of trees, using their spine-tipped tails as props.

WHERE THEY LIVE: Verdins live in deserts with thorny trees, brush, and cactuses. They build a series of large, round nests, most of which are used only for roosting. Brown Creepers are forest and woodland birds. Their nests are built behind flakes of bark on dead or dying trees.

WHAT THEY EAT: Invertebrates, including caterpillars, aphids, and spiders. Verdins also eat fruit, drink flower nectar, and sometimes visit hummingbird feeders.

SOUNDS: The robust chips and plaintive whistle of Verdins are common sounds in their habitat. Creepers have high, thin voices, almost beyond the range of human hearing.

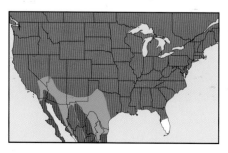

● **Range where Brown Creepers are found.**
● **Range where Verdins are found.**
● **Range where both Brown Creepers and Verdins are found.**

Opposite: Verdin. *Above:* Brown Creeper.

Nuthatches   No. of species: 4

SIZE: 4 to 6 inches

HOW TO KNOW THEM: Compact little birds with short tails, large heads and long bills, nuthatches are built to cling. Their strong feet and sharp claws allow them to move almost any direction on the trunks and limbs of trees, even upside down. All have gray backs and white throats. The Red-breasted Nuthatch as named for its rusty cinnamon underparts.

WHERE THEY LIVE: Forests and woodlands. The most widespread species, the White-breasted, lives in deciduous woodlands and mixed broad-leaf/conifer forests. Red-breasted Nuthatches prefer conifer forests with fir and spruce. Brown-headed and Pygmy Nuthatches live in pine forests on opposite sides of the continent.

WHAT THEY EAT: Insects, spiders, seeds. The name "nuthatch" may have been inspired by the birds' habit of wedging nuts and other large seeds in bark crevices before hammering them open.

SOUNDS: Nasal beeps, chirps, and yelps. The voice of the Red-breasted Nuthatch has been compared to the sound of a tin horn.

ETC.: Though not migratory, the Red-breasted Nuthatch sometimes undergoes "irruptions" in which large numbers invade regions and habitats outside their normal range. Nuthatches sometimes use flakes of bark as tools to pry up other bark flakes.

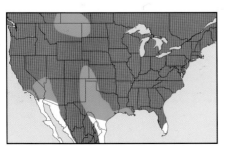

● Range of nuthatches in winter.
◑ Range where nuthatches are found all year.

Opposite: Red-breasted Nuthatch. ***Above:*** White-breasted Nuthatch.

Wrens No. of species: 9

SIZE: 4 to 9 inches

HOW TO KNOW THEM: Wrens are small, active birds with short, rounded wings, and tails that are often cocked upright. Most species have cryptic brown coloration and a tendency to inhabit dense thickets, making them difficult to observe. Their long, thin bills are well adapted for gleaning insects from trees, rocks, and leaves.

WHERE THEY LIVE: Dense thickets from river bottom forest to desert scrub and rocky canyons. The tiny Winter Wren depends primarily on old growth forests.

WHAT THEY EAT: Predominately insects and other invertebrates, some berries and other fruits, seeds, and eggs of other birds. Appropriately enough, Cactus Wrens feed on the juicy red-purple fruits of saguaro and prickly pear cactuses.

SOUNDS: Their loud, harsh scolding calls and powerful, sweet songs belie their small size, but wrens also whine, snarl, and chip. The songs of Carolina Wrens sound like a rapid "teakettle-teakettle-teakettle." The flute-like, descending notes of Canyon Wrens are among the most evocative sounds of the West.

ETC.: The Winter Wren, the only member of its family found in Europe, is a prominent character in fable and folklore.

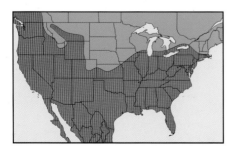

● **Range of wrens in summer.**
◍ **Range where wrens are found all year.**

Opposite: Carolina Wren. ***Above:*** Bewick's Wren. ***Above inset:*** Marsh Wren.

Wrentit & Dippers No. of species: 1 + 1

SIZE: 7 to 8 inches

HOW TO KNOW THEM: Though not closely related to either wrens or titmice, secretive Wrentits combine some of the physical and behavioral characteristics of the two groups. Their yellow eyes are the only bright color on otherwise drab gray-brown birds. American Dippers are songbirds that dive like seabirds, using their wings to "fly" underwater. Their dull brown and slate gray plumage is enlivened by bright white eyelids that flash when the birds blink. The name comes from their compulsive "dipping," bobbing the entire body up and down.

WHERE THEY LIVE: Wrentits are found in chaparral habitats from Baja California to western Oregon. Dippers live along clear, cold streams throughout western North America, building their nests nearby.

WHAT THEY EAT: Wrentits feed on insects, spiders, fruits, and seeds. Dippers feed mainly on aquatic insects and their larvae, small fish, fish eggs, and tadpoles.

SOUNDS: The Wrentit is known as the "voice of the chaparral" for its bright monotone trill. American Dippers sing a sweet song of varied wren-like phrases. In both species males and females sing year round.

ETC.: Wrentit pairs form strong, lifelong bonds.

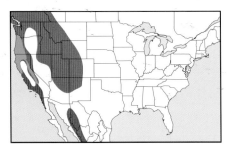

● Range where Wrentits are found all year.
● Range where American Dippers are found all year.
● Range where both Wrentits and American Dippers are found all year.

Opposite: Wrentit. ***Above:*** American Dipper.

Kinglets & Gnatcatchers No. of species: 2 + 4

SIZE: 4 to 5 inches

HOW TO KNOW THEM: Vivid color patches on the crown as well as a bold and haughty personality earned the kinglets their name. These colors — a splash of bright red on male Ruby-crowneds, bands of black, white, yellow and orange on Golden-crowneds — are seen mainly when the birds are agitated. Gnatcatchers lack such adornments, but these tiny gray birds have long, expressive tails boldly patterned in black and white. Both are very active foragers, in nearly constant motion as they glean insects from foliage and bark.

WHERE THEY LIVE: Forests, woodlands, chaparral, shrubby deserts. Though seldom seen in the remote spruce-fir forests where they nest, kinglets winter in a variety of habitats through much of the United States. Blue-gray Gnatcatcher is the only gnatcatcher found in the East.

WHAT THEY EAT: Insects, spiders and other invertebrates, small berries. Tail wagging is thought to help the gnatcatchers flush prey from hiding.

SOUNDS: Kinglets sing brisk, bouncy songs of varied phrases, mostly from spring through summer. Their call note, heard throughout the year, is a harsh "chi-dit." Gnatcatchers sing a buzzy, peevish song and give a plaintive kitten-like mew.

ETC.: California Gnatcatchers, only recently recognized as a distinct species, are endangered due to habitat destruction.

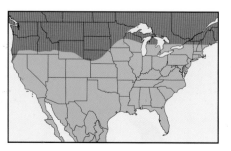

● **Range where kinglets are found.**

● **Range where both kinglets and gnatcatchers are found.**

Opposite: Golden-crowned Kinglet. ***Above:*** Black-tailed Gnatcatcher.

Thrushes No. of species: 16

SIZE: 6 to 10 inches

HOW TO KNOW THEM: Thrushes are medium-sized to large songbirds that include some of our most familiar birds as well as some of our most secretive. Their common traits include large, dark eyes, upright posture, and slender bills. The reclusive "spotted thrushes" — brown above with dark-spotted white underparts — prefer deep forests and are far less familiar than are robins and bluebirds (covered on subsequent pages). These birds skulk along the forest floor, tossing aside leaf litter in search of prey. The most colorful and least shy member of this group, the Wood Thrush, enlivens suburban gardens and city parks with its lovely flute-like song.

WHERE THEY LIVE: Forests, woodlands, grasslands, and farm country. Most thrushes in the United States are migratory and many spotted thrushes leave North America entirely in winter. A notable exception is the Hermit Thrush, which can be found throughout the winter in warmer parts of the United States.

WHAT THEY EAT: Insects, other invertebrates, and fruit.

SOUNDS: Thrushes are famous for their songs, especially the ethereal songs of spotted thrushes.

ETC.: The Wood Thrush epitomizes the plight of neotropical migrants. It faces threats from habitat destruction on both its breeding grounds in the eastern United States and wintering grounds in Mexico and Central America.

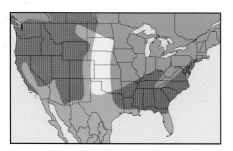

- Range of thrushes in migration.
- **Range of thrushes in summer.**
- **Range of thrushes in winter.**
- **Range where thrushes are found all year.**

Opposite: Swainson's Thrush. **Above:** Hermit Thrush.

Robins No. of species: 3

SIZE: 9 to 10 inches.

HOW TO KNOW THEM: The American Robin is one of our most familiar songbirds. With their reddish-orange breasts, whitish eye-rings, and gray-brown backs, they are easy to recognize. The Clay-colored Robin of far southern Texas and Mexico resembles a drab version of its northern cousin.

WHERE THEY LIVE: American Robins are quite comfortable around people and they can be found in urban parks and suburban neighborhoods as well as in meadows and forests across most of the continent. Though in the northern reaches of their range the arrival of robins is a harbinger of spring, in most of the United States they are present year round.

WHAT THEY EAT: Mainly insects and earthworms in spring and summer, switching to fruits in fall and winter. Robins cock their heads from side to side while foraging, probably to detect the faint movements of their prey.

SOUNDS: The cheerful dawn chorus of American Robins is music to a birder's ears, but may be less welcome for those who would prefer not to wake at sunrise.

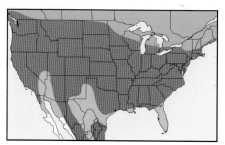

ETC.: The robins of the New World are not closely related to the European Robin, a small, migratory flycatcher. Both have red breasts and the superficial similarity led American settlers to use the same name.

- Range of robins in summer.
- Range of robins in winter.
- Range where robins are found all year.

Opposite: American Robin at nest. ***Above:*** American Robin.
Above inset: American Robin with captured worm.

Bluebirds No. of species: 3

SIZE: 7 inches

HOW TO KNOW THEM: Their bright blue color, on birds larger than warblers and smaller than jays, says bluebird. Buntings (page 218), and grosbeaks (page 216) have much chunkier bills.

WHERE THEY LIVE: Open woodlands, farmlands, and meadows.

WHAT THEY EAT: Mainly insects, but also fruits and seeds.

SOUNDS: A soft warble, sometimes sounding like "truly, truly."

ETC.: The Eastern Bluebird is an icon of happiness, and these birds had plenty to sing about in the 19th century as settlement and clearing of forests for farming created abundant new habitat. By the middle of the 20th century, that trend had turned around, and bluebirds slipped into a severe decline across the eastern United States. Bluebird aficionados intervened on the birds' behalf, initiating nest-box programs to replace natural cavities lost to changes in farming and forestry practices. Hundreds of miles of "bluebird trails" helped bring Eastern Bluebirds back to many areas from which they had disappeared. Western and Mountain Bluebirds also have bene-fitted from nest boxes. Eastern Bluebirds are admired as models of wholesome, peaceful family life, but the real story is more like a soap opera. Territorial squabbles are sometimes fatal, and males often unwittingly raise young that are not their own.

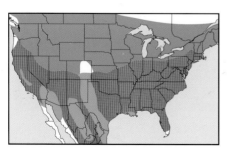

● **Range of bluebirds in summer.**
● **Range of bluebirds in winter.**
● **Range where bluebirds are found all year.**

Opposite: Female Western Bluebird. ***Above:*** Male Eastern Bluebird. Above inset: Mountain Bluebird.

Catbirds & Mockingbirds No. of species: 1 + 1

SIZE: 9 to 10 inches

HOW TO KNOW THEM: What catbirds and mockingbirds lack in colorful plumage they make up for with their extraordinary voices. These fine mimics are among the virtuosos of the bird world, able to incorporate a variety of sounds into their repertoires. The catbird's jaunty black "beret" and chestnut undertail coverts make it unique among North American birds. Mockingbirds use white flashes in their wings and tail as semaphores during their territorial displays.

WHERE THEY LIVE: Catbirds can be heard in woodland thickets and hedges over much of the United States in summer, while the Northern Mockingbird is a conspicuous year-round resident of suburbs and parks as well as natural woodland habitats over most of its wide range.

WHAT THEY EAT: Insects, other invertebrates, fruit.

SOUNDS: The full range of these versatile vocalists would be impossible to describe. The catbird takes its name from its nasal mewing call note. The mockingbird's most common call is a harsh "chack."

ETC.: Full moons and street lights often inspire mockingbirds, especially unpaired males, to nocturnal serenades. A catbird can perform a duet with itself, singing different phrases from each side of its paired vocal apparatus.

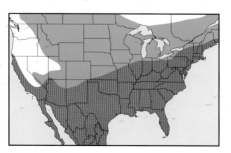

⬤ Range of catbirds and mockingbirds in summer.
◐ Range where catbirds and mockingbirds are found all year.

Opposite: Gray Catbird. **Above:** Northern Mockingbird.

Thrashers No. of species: 8

SIZE: 9 to 12 inches

HOW TO KNOW THEM: These long-legged, slim, medium-sized songbirds are named for their energetic foraging behavior, tossing aside leaf litter, twigs, and stones in search of food items. Most of their time is spent on the ground or hidden away in dense vegetation. Their plumage is generally gray to rusty brown, with spots or streaks on the breast. Bills vary from relatively short and straight in the Sage Thrasher to extravagantly long and decurved in the California Thrasher.

WHERE THEY LIVE: The eastern Brown Thrasher prefers brushland and woodland edges. Western thrashers prefer more open habitats such as sagebrush, chaparral, and thorny desert thickets.

WHAT THEY EAT: Fruit, seeds, insects and other invertebrates, with proportions varying by season and habitat.

SOUNDS: Like mockingbirds, their close relatives, thrashers have varied and complex vocal repertoires and are accomplished mimics. The loud "wheet-wheet" of the Curve-billed Thrasher is a signature sound of the Southwest. Thrashers often sing early in the morning from a conspicuous perch.

ETC.: Like mockingbirds, thrashers can be very aggressive toward potential predators, even attacking animals much larger than themselves.

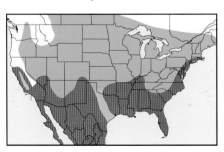

● **Range of thrashers in summer.**
● **Range of thrashers in winter.**
◉ **Range where thrashers are found all year.**

Opposite: Brown Thrasher. ***Above:*** Sage Thrasher.

Starlings No. of species: 3 (all introduced)

SIZE: 9 inches

HOW TO KNOW THEM: European Starlings are medium-sized songbirds with strong legs and long, narrow bills. In fall, pale feather tips obscure the shiny black plumage. By spring, these tips wear away to reveal satiny green and purple iridescences. The bill also changes color, turning from blackish to bright yellow. Escaped cage birds, Common and Hill Mynas, well-established only in south Florida, have yellow skin around their eyes and white wing patches.

WHERE THEY LIVE: Virtually everywhere, from city parks to feedlots and farm fields.

WHAT THEY EAT: Cosmopolitan tastes are one key to the starling's success. They will eat almost any food available, including seeds, insects, earthworms, fruit, crops, livestock feed, and garbage.

SOUNDS: A variety of harsh screeches and chatters. Starlings are accomplished mimics, often learning human and mechanical sounds as well as those of other birds.

ETC.: European Starlings were released in New York City's Central Park in 1890 and 1891 in a misguided attempt to establish in the United States all the birds mentioned by Shakespeare. From approximately one hundred birds we now have a population of approximately two hundred million starlings in North America. They compete with native birds for food, nesting cavities, and other resources.

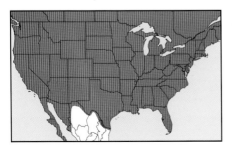

● **Range where starlings are found all year.**

Opposite: Common Myna. ***Above:*** European Starling. ***Above inset:*** Flock of European Starlings.

Pipits & Wagtails No. of species: 3 + 1

SIZE: 6 to 7 inches

HOW TO KNOW THEM: These slender birds of open country spend much of their time on the ground. They have long legs, long tails, and a small pointed bill. The pipits are generally streaked with brown to blend in with the grasses of their open country home. American Pipits winter in flocks and are most often seen as they fly low over grassland, plowed fields, or beaches. Though similar in plumage to Horned Larks, and many sparrows, American Pipits walk with a tail-bobbing motion. Similar behavior is seen in the wagtails, boldly marked songbirds that are rarely seen south of Alaska.

WHERE THEY LIVE: Open country, such as alpine and arctic tundra, high meadows, and prairies in summer; prairies, desert grasslands, marshes, mud flats, coastal beaches, and farm fields in migration and winter. The solitary, secretive, and declining Sprague's Pipit of the central plains requires undisturbed native grasslands for nesting.

WHAT THEY EAT: Seeds, arthropods, and insects. American Pipits search shorelines for aquatic insect larvae, even wading into shallow water to feed.

SOUNDS: Male pipits sing in flight over their territories. Flight calls of migrating and wintering flocks are a faint tinkling sound.

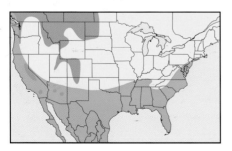

- Range of pipits in migration.
- **Range of pipits in summer.**
- **Range of pipits in winter.**

Opposite: Yellow Wagtail. *Above:* Sprague's Pipit. *Above inset:* American Pipit.

Waxwings & Phainopepla No. of species: 2 + 1

SIZE: 8 inches

HOW TO KNOW THEM: Sleek and crested, these birds share an affinity for berries. Waxwings are gregarious, often gathering in large flocks. With their elegant crests, yellow-tipped tails, and waxy red accents on the wings, they seem impeccably groomed. Phainopeplas, members of a tropical family known as silky-flycatchers, are slim, long-tailed birds of the southwestern deserts. Males are shiny black, females are charcoal grey. Both sexes have spiky crests, bright red eyes, and broad white wing patches.

WHERE THEY LIVE: Waxwings are widespread wherever berry bushes are found. Movements of populations are tied to berry crops. Phainopeplas are found in mountain foothills and deserts of the Southwest.

WHAT THEY EAT: Fruit and insects. The Phainopepla specializes in mistletoe berries.

SOUNDS: Waxwings constantly twitter with a very high pitched chatter, while Phainopeplas make a plaintive, questioning, "wherp?"

ETC.: Waxwings are named for waxy red tips on their inner wing feathers. Phainopeplas nest in two different habitats at different times: in early spring in the desert scrub and in summer in the mountains. It is unclear whether the same individuals nest twice in a year.

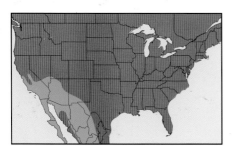

● **Range of waxwings.**
● **Range where both waxwings and Phainopeplas are found.**

Opposite: Bohemian Waxwing. ***Above:*** Cedar Waxwing. ***Above inset:*** Phainopepla.

Wood-Warblers No. of species: 52 (1 extinct)

SIZE: 4 to 7 inches

HOW TO KNOW THEM: Perhaps no other group of birds is as varied in plumage color and patterns as the warblers. The "typical" warbler might be thought of as a small bird with some yellow and a thin, sharp bill, but the extravagant diversity of the group makes any generalization of little value. Three species, including Black-and-white Warbler, are black and white. Three other species look similar to the Black-throated Green Warbler, while many species, with blue-gray color on their backs and black-streaked yellow on their breasts, loosely resemble the Magnolia Warbler shown on page 201. Adult males in breeding plumage are often unmistakable, but seasonal and age-related changes in appearance offer many identification challenges. Females, usually duller than males, and immature birds on their first fall migration, can be especially difficult. Although some warblers may be found in bushes, or even in open country, most individuals will be seen in the tree-tops, where they rarely stay still. This constant movement in the tree canopy is a clue to the bird's identity as a warbler. In size, warblers range from drab and diminutive Lucy's Warblers (4 inches) to chunky Yellow-breasted Chats (7 inches).

(*continued on page 198*)

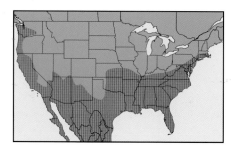

● **Range of warblers in summer.**

◍ **Range where warblers are found all year.**

Opposite: Unlike other warblers, Black-and-white Warblers feed by clambering along tree trunks and large limbs. ***Above:*** Black-throated Green Warbler

Wood-Warblers (*continued*)

WHERE THEY LIVE: Many habitats, including forests, woodlands, desert scrub, swamps, and marshes. Most warblers build open cup nests in a tree or shrub (see page 25), but some species nest on the ground, and Lucy's Warbler nests in tree cavities. Warblers have been so successful in part because of their ability to specialize in a particular habitat or feeding niche. Many different warbler species may inhabit the same patch of forest or woodland, with one species specializing in feeding on the ground, another in the understory, another on the lower branches of the canopy, and yet another species feeding mainly at the tips of the outermost branches.

WHAT THEY EAT: Insects and other invertebrates. Most warblers live in the tree canopy, gleaning prey from foliage or catching flying insects in midair. The perky Black-and-white Warbler clings to tree trunks like a zebra-backed nuthatch, probing for insects hidden in bark crevices.

SOUNDS: Calls are mostly chip-notes, varying by species from sweet to harsh. Songs range from simple insect-like trills to complex series of alternating phrases. Common and widespread Common Yellowthroats sing "witchity, witchity, witchity" while Blue-winged Warblers sing "bee-bomb," with the second note lower.

(*continued on page 200*)

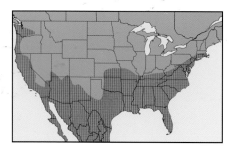

● **Range of warblers in summer.**
◉ **Range where warblers are found all year.**

Opposite: Common Yellowthroat. ***Above:*** Chestnut-sided Warbler. ***Above inset:*** Black-throated Blue Warbler.

Wood-Warblers (*continued*)

ETC.: The huge waves of warblers in spring migration are one of the highlights of the birding year. In some areas, on big migrations days, more than thirty species of these sparkling jewels can be seen in a single morning. Unfortunately, the staggering numbers so characteristic of these migrations in the past has declined. Many warblers are pressured by changes in available habitat not only on their summer breeding grounds, but also in their tropical wintering range.

Many warblers have suffered as forests were cleared, but the Chestnut-sided Warbler thrives in sunny edges and brushy second growth and has increased its range and population. The bandit-masked Common Yellowthroat has also prospered by embracing a wide range of habitats, from pine forests and shrubby streamside thickets to cattail marshes.

Kirtland's Warbler of Michigan and Golden-cheeked Warbler of central Texas are endangered because their extremely limited habitats are threatened by human activities. Kirtland's Warblers breed only in stands of young jack pines that grow following forest fires. Suppression of natural fires degraded its habitat, causing populations to plummet to only a few hundred individuals. Prescribed fires and control of nest-parasitizing cowbirds have helped the species rebound.

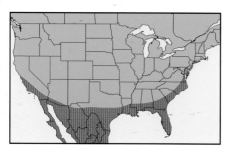

Golden-cheeked Warblers depend upon oak-juniper woodlands that are rapidly being destroyed and degraded by agriculture and urban sprawl.

● **Range of Common Yellowthroats in summer.**
◉ **Range where Common Yellowthroats are found all year.**

Opposite: Blue-winged Warbler. ***Above:*** Magnolia Warbler. ***Above inset:*** American Redstart.

Tanagers — No. of species: 5

SIZE: 7 to 8 inches

HOW TO KNOW THEM: These medium-sized forest birds have strong bills and spectacular male plumage. The bodies of adult males are vivid red, orange or yellow, accented in the Scarlet and Western Tanagers by black wings. Females are solely responsible for incubating the eggs and brooding the young, and their muted colors help to avoid drawing attention to the nest.

WHERE THEY LIVE: Broadleaf and conifer forests and woodlands. The survival of Scarlet Tanager populations depends upon large tracts of intact forest. Patches less than thirty acres in size expose nesting birds to increased predation and nest parasitism by cowbirds. All tanagers are long-distance migrants, leaving the United States entirely in winter.

WHAT THEY EAT: A variety of insects, including significant numbers of bees, wasps, and hornets, spiders, snails, earthworms, and fruits such as mulberries and chokecherries.

SOUNDS: Calls are loud and percussive, usually consisting of two or three hoarse notes slurred together. Songs are a stuttery series of sweet to buzzy phrases. Males often sing from high, conspicuous perches.

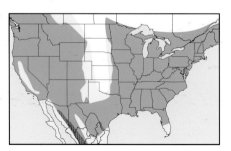

ETC.: In fall, male Scarlet Tanagers undergo a partial molt in which their brilliant red head and body plumage is replaced with dull yellow-green feathers.

⬤ Range of tanagers in migration.

⬤ Range of tanagers in summer.

⬤ Range where tanagers are found all year.

Opposite: Western Tanager. **Above:** Male Scarlet Tanager. **Above inset:** Female Summer Tanager.

Towhees No. of species: 6

SIZE: 7 to 9 inches

HOW TO KNOW THEM: Towhees, part of the sparrow family, are medium-sized ground-hugging birds that represent the extremes of color variation in sparrows. Closely related Eastern and Spotted Towhees are gaudy birds from their rusty vests and dark "hoods" to their red eyes. Three similar-looking western species, Canyon, California, and Abert's Towhees, have plumages that match the dusty soil and dry brush of their desert and chaparral habitats.

WHERE THEY LIVE: Brushy thickets, forest and woodland understory, desert scrub, and arid grasslands. In most area, towhees are resident. Only the Green-tailed Towhee has completely different summer and winter ranges.

WHAT THEY EAT: Insects and other invertebrates, seeds, and fruits. Towhees kick and scratch in the leaf litter to uncover seeds and insects.

SOUNDS: Include chatters, chips, and trills. Eastern Towhees make a nasal "chewink" call and sing a slurred "drink your teeeeeeee," Spotted Towhees make a nasal, cat-like mreer and sing "drink drink teeeeeeee."

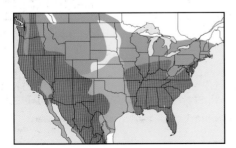

● Range of towhees in migration.
● Range of towhees in summer.
● Range of towhees in winter.
◑ Range where towhees are found all year.

Opposite left: California Towhee. **Opposite right:** Green-tailed Towhee. **Top:** Eastern Towhee. **Bottom:** Spotted Towhee.

Typical Sparrows No. of species: 33

SIZE: 5 to 8 inches

HOW TO KNOW THEM: These small to medium-sized birds, whose variegated brown to grayish plumage provide excellent camouflage, are usually found on or near the ground, rather than high in trees. Their bills are short and conical. The Chipping Sparrow is one of the smallest species, while the handsomely marked White-crowned Sparrow and variably attired Fox Sparrow are two of the largest. Most species are quietly colored through all ages and seasons, but a few don brighter plumage for the breeding season. This can be as subtle as the rusty cap of male and female Chipping Sparrows or as gaudy as the satiny black and white plumage of a male Lark Bunting, which, despite its name, is a sparrow.

WHERE THEY LIVE: Everywhere in North America, from arctic tundra and mountain slopes to suburban gardens to deserts and seaside marshes. Some species are restricted to particular habitats while others are much more flexible in their requirements. For example, Black-throated Sparrows are normally only found in deserts, while widespread Song Sparrows may be seen in deserts, brushy thickets, marshes, suburban gardens, and second-growth woodlands.

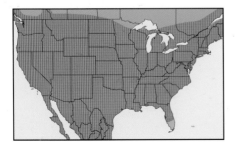

WHAT THEY EAT: Seeds are dietary staples year round for many species, but insects are vitally important during nesting season.

(*continued on page 208*)

- ● Range of typical sparrows in summer.
- ● Range of typical sparrows in winter.
- ◉ Range where typical sparrows are found all year.

Opposite: White-crowned Sparrow. **Above:** White-throated Sparrow singing.
Above inset: Black-throated Sparrow.

Typical Sparrows (*continued*)

SOUNDS: A variety of pleasing chips and trills. The song of the White-throated Sparrow sounds like "o-o-old sa-a-am peabody peabody peabody." Similar White-crowned Sparrows have well-defined regional "dialects" that males memorize long before their first attempts to sing. Sparrows sing from a variety of positions. Some species sing from the top of a bush, some, such as Vesper Sparrows, sing while on the ground, while other sparrows sing in flight, a behavior known as "skylarking." In some species, such as Grasshopper Sparrow, both males and females sing.

GEOGRAPHIC VARIATION: Some widespread sparrow species have formed distinct regional populations. The eighteen subspecies of the Fox Sparrow vary from rich chestnut red in northern and eastern populations to chocolate brown in the Pacific Northwest and Alaska. The ubiquitous Song Sparrow is considered one of the most variable birds in the world; at least two dozen subspecies can be distinguished on the basis of size and plumage color.

MIGRATION: Some sparrows are long-distance migrants, while others are more habitat-specific and seldom stray far from home. American Tree Sparrows nest in arctic and subarctic habitats and winter in the northern two-thirds of the United States. They migrate at night, using polarized light at dusk to orient themselves southward in fall and northward in spring.

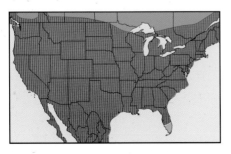

● Range of typical sparrows in summer.
● Range of typical sparrows in winter.
● Range where typical sparrows are found all year.

Opposite: American Tree Sparrow. ***Above:*** Fox Sparrow. ***Above inset:*** Grasshopper Sparrow.

Juncos & Longspurs No. of species: 2 + 4

SIZE: 6 to 7 inches

HOW TO KNOW THEM: These atypical sparrows flash their bright white outer tail feathers as the flock scatters at your approach. Juncos are familiar feeder birds, often called "snowbirds" for their tendency to appear during or after winter storms. Their plumage is mostly smooth slate gray to gray-brown, with wide variation in color and pattern. Longspurs are ground-hugging open-country sparrows, usually found in large flocks. They have short legs and colorful breeding plumage in the males. Two of the longspurs nest on tundra, two on prairies, but all four winter together in the southern plains.

WHERE THEY LIVE: Coniferous forests and woodlands, prairies, and arctic tundra in summer, woodlands, prairies, deserts, farmlands, and suburban yards in winter.

WHAT THEY EAT: Invertebrates, including pests such as spruce budworms, grass and weed seeds, some fruits and other vegetable matter.

SOUNDS: Chips, trills, whistles, and twitters similar to those of other sparrows.

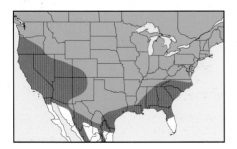

● **Range of juncos.**
● **Range where both juncos and longspurs are found.**

Opposite left: Lapland Longspur. ***Opposite right:*** Yellow-eyed Junco. ***Above:*** Dark-eyed Junco (Slate-colored subspecies). ***Above inset:*** Dark-eyed Junco (Oregon subspecies).

Cardinals No. of species: 2

SIZE: 8 inches

HOW TO KNOW THEM: The Northern Cardinal is one of the most beloved songbirds in North America. The male's scarlet plumage has adorned countless holiday cards, collector plates, T-shirts, and other decorative items. Both sexes can be recognized by their red color, crests, and conical red bills, but the plumage of females is much more subdued. Young birds have dark bills. Its less gaudy southwestern cousin, the Pyrrhuloxia, shares many of its traits, including songs and calls, but is primarily gray.

WHERE THEY LIVE: Thickets, hedgerows, desert scrub, and shrubby suburban landscapes.

WHAT THEY EAT: Seeds, especially hard-shelled varieties inaccessible to smaller-billed birds, insects, and other invertebrates.

SOUNDS: Many songs, including the familiar "cheer cheer cheer," as well as hard, metallic chips and clear, slurred whistles. Unlike many birds, cardinals sing throughout the year.

ETC.: Mated cardinals often remain together throughout the year. Once primarily southern, over the past fifty years cardinals have moved into much of the northern United States. The cardinal family includes the grosbeaks and tropical buntings, covered on subsequent pages.

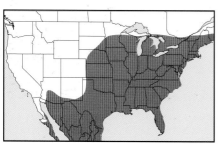

🔴 **Range where cardinals are found all year.**

Opposite: Female Northern Cardinal. **Above:** Male Northern Cardinal.

Grosbeaks No. of species: 3

SIZE: 7 to 8 inches

HOW TO KNOW THEM: Rose-breasted, Black-headed, and Blue Grosbeaks are close relatives of cardinals. Rose-breasted and Black-headed Grosbeaks are stocky birds with large heads and formidable bills. Males have colorful breasts and bright black and white wing and tail patterns. Females resemble oversized sparrows, complete with face and crown stripes and streaked brown backs and wings. Blue Grosbeak are very similar to tropical buntings (see following pages) except for their slightly larger size and stout bill.

WHERE THEY LIVE: Rose-breasted and Black-headed Grosbeaks nest in hardwood forests and woodlands, while Blue Grosbeaks prefer more open country, including streamside thickets, brushy meadows, and woodland edges.

WHAT THEY EAT: Large, hard seeds, insects, berries, and other fruits. In late summer, mulberries are important foods for Rose-breasted and Black-headed Grosbeaks.

SOUNDS: Melodious warbling songs, hard nasal or metallic call notes. In Rose-breasted and Black-headed grosbeaks, both sexes sing, even while incubating eggs.

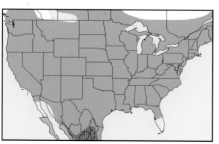

ETC.: Evening and Pine Grosbeaks are oversized finches and are not closely related to these grosbeaks.

- Range of grosbeaks in migration.
- Range of grosbeaks in summer.
- Range of grosbeaks in winter.
- Range where grosbeaks are found all year.

Opposite: Blue Grosbeak. **Above:** Rose-breasted Grosbeak.

Tropical Buntings No. of species: 5

SIZE: 6 inches

HOW TO KNOW THEM: These small songbirds are among the most beautiful birds in the world. The sky blue head of a male Lazuli Bunting or the palette of colors on a Painted Bunting seem almost artificial. The muted green or brown colors of the females help to conceal them as they incubate the eggs.

WHERE THEY LIVE: Grassy fields, woody streamside thickets, shrubby woodland edges in summer, pastures, weedy fields, and tropical forest edges in winter. Nests are cups of grasses, leaves, and bark built close to the ground in shrubs or low trees.

WHAT THEY EAT: Primarily insects during the breeding season, seeds in winter.

SOUNDS: All species make sharp metallic chip notes. Songs, sung only by males, are high-pitched bouncy warbles, often with certain phrases repeated two or three times.

ETC.: Despite complete protection from commercial exploitation in the United States, the buntings are still trapped on their tropical wintering grounds to be sold as cage birds. The Painted Bunting is on the National Audubon Society's Watch List; its small breeding range compared to other buntings makes it especially vulnerable to both habitat destruction and exploitation by the pet trade.

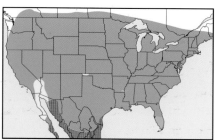

Range of buntings in migration.
Range of buntings in summer.
Range of buntings in winter.
Range where buntings are found all year.

Opposite: Indigo Bunting. **Above:** Lazuli Bunting. **Above inset:** Painted Bunting.

Meadowlarks & Bobolink No. of species: 2 + 1

SIZE: 7 to 10 inches

HOW TO KNOW THEM: Meadowlarks are not larks at all but large, quail-like members of the blackbird family. Their bright yellow breast with black V and brown-streaked back are familiar to residents of the Midwest and Great Plains. Meadowlarks can choose to be conspicuous with bright breast showing or can crouch low to the ground showing only the finely streaked back, well camouflaged against the grass. The Bobolink, a sparrow-like blackbird, has earned the nickname "skunk blackbird" for the unusual pale-above, black-below breeding plumage of the adult male.

WHERE THEY LIVE: Prairie and open fields, agricultural lands. The Bobolink is highly migratory. It spends its summers in the northern United States and southern Canada and its winters in central South America, a round trip of over 12,000 miles.

WHAT THEY EAT: Weed and grass seeds, grasshoppers, grubs, and other invertebrates.

SOUNDS: Western Meadowlark's rich flute-like song helps to distinguish it from the similar-looking Eastern Meadowlark, whose song is a thin whistle.

ETC.: The Western Meadowlark's exquisite song inspired residents of six central and western states to adopt it as their state bird. The Eastern Meadowlark has received no such honors.

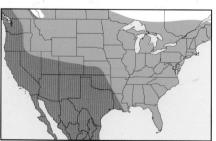

● **Range where meadowlarks are found.**
● **Range where both meadowlarks and Bobolinks are found.**

Opposite: Bobolink. ***Above:*** Western Meadowlark.

Blackbirds No. of species: 11

SIZE: 8 to 18 inches

HOW TO KNOW THEM: The "true" blackbirds are a more colorful group than the name implies. Though black and dark brown are predominant colors, a few sport vivid plumage accents of red and yellow while others have conspicuous yellow or red eyes and subtle iridescence. Females are less intensely colored than males or even dramatically different, as in the Red-winged Blackbird. They range from the sparrow-sized Brown-headed Cowbird to the nearly crow-sized Great-tailed Grackle. Most are noisy and gregarious, with winter flocks sometimes numbering in the millions.

WHERE THEY LIVE: Wetlands, agricultural areas, feedlots, urban areas. Widespread.

WHAT THEY EAT: Grass seeds, waste grain, wide variety of insects and other invertebrates. The adaptable Great-tailed Grackle also feeds on small vertebrates, crustaceans, garbage, carrion, and pet food.

SOUNDS: Blackbirds are enthusiastic vocalists, though their songs are not always pleasant to the human ear. The shrill congaree song of the Red-winged Blackbird is emblematic of wetlands throughout the United States.

ETC.: Cowbirds are nest parasites, laying eggs in other birds' nests. This successful adaptation to a nomadic lifestyle has had a devastating effect on populations of other songbirds.

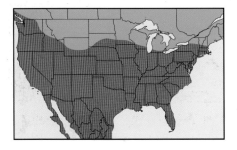

● **Range of blackbirds in summer.**
● **Range where blackbirds are found all year.**

Opposite: Brown-headed Cowbird. **Above:** Male Red-winged Blackbird. **Above inset:** Female Red-winged Blackbird.

Orioles   No. of species: 8

SIZE: 7 to 10 inches

HOW TO KNOW THEM: The most colorful members of the blackbird family, orioles are medium-sized birds with yellow or orange and black plumage and long, thin bills. They are famous for their exquisitely woven hanging nests, which range in size from a deep cup to a long enclosed pouch. Females are generally less colorful than males except in the Altamira Oriole of extreme southern Texas and the Spot-breasted Oriole, a Central American species introduced to Florida.

WHERE THEY LIVE: A variety of woodland, forest, and desert habitats throughout the Lower 48 states in summer; tropical forests, shrub thickets, and woodland edges from southernmost Texas south in winter.

WHAT THEY EAT: Fruits, nectar, caterpillars, grasshoppers, ants, boll weevils, spiders, snails, and other invertebrates. Orioles are apparently important pollinators in the tropics. Scott's Orioles eat Monarchs at their winter roosts in central Mexico, having apparently learned how to select and consume the butterflies' less toxic parts.

SOUNDS: Beautiful flute-like songs, harsh scolding call notes, nasal whistles.

ETC.: Orioles tend to be shy but can be attracted to feeding stations by offering oranges, bananas, grapes, and other soft fruits.

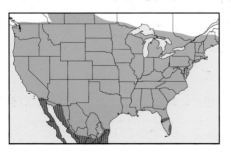

● **Range of orioles in summer.**
● **Range of orioles in winter.**
⦿ **Range where orioles are found all year.**

Opposite: Scott's Oriole. ***Above:*** Baltimore Oriole.

Finches   No. of species: 16

SIZE: 5 to 9 inches

HOW TO KNOW THEM: These small to medium-sized songbirds have cone-shaped bills that are specialized for feeding on seeds. Males of most species have a reddish hue as the major color of their plumage and females tend to have a similar, but browner, pattern. The majority of finches fly with a characteristic undulating flight. One is more likely to see a flock of finches than a single individual. The House Finch is one of the most variable of our native birds, ranging from brown to yellow to red depending on age, sex, and health. The largest bills in this group belong to the Evening and Pine Grosbeaks, which are actually large finches.

WHERE THEY LIVE: Woodland edges, weedy meadows, hardwood and conifer forests, deserts, alpine and arctic tundra. The rosy-finches are high-elevation species adapted to life above timberline, while dainty redpolls nest in the arctic.

WHAT THEY EAT: Seeds, fruits, buds, insects. Sunflower seeds are a favorite of many finches. Many of the species feed on the ground, but crossbills specialize in extracting the seeds from the cones of pines and other conifers.

(*continued on page 226*)

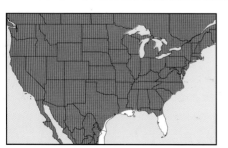

⬤ **Range where finches are found all year.**

Opposite: Common Redpoll. **Above:** Male House Finch. **Above inset:** Female House Finch.

Finches (*continued*)

SOUNDS: A variety of calls and songs, some quite musical.

ETC.: House Finches were once captured in California and sold in the East as cage birds ("Hollywood finches" or "red linnets") before legal protection for all our songbirds was established. The eastern population of House Finches is descended from former cage birds released in the late 1940s, after passage of the law. The expanding eastern population has joined with expanding native populations in the West, resulting in a continent-wide range for the species. Depending upon the particular winter, many species of northern finches, including crossbills, redpolls, and grosbeaks, may migrate more or less farther south. A finch "irruption" year is an exciting event for many birders and adds color to many winter feeders. In winters when the supply of fruits and seeds becomes unusually low in the north country, Pine Grosbeaks and Evening Grosbeaks may leave their traditional Canadian wintering grounds and visit much of the northeastern United States or, in the case of Evening Grosbeaks, even the southeastern states.

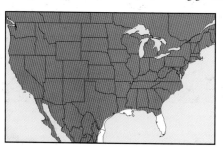

● **Range where finches are found all year.**

Opposite: Red Crossbill. **Above:** Evening Grosbeak.

Goldfinches and Siskins No. of species: 4

SIZE: 4 to 5 inches

HOW TO KNOW THEM: Goldfinches and siskins are tiny yellowish finches with white or yellow wing markings and tiny, thin bills adapted for extracting seeds from tight spaces. The male American Goldfinch undergoes a dramatic transformation each spring, exchanging khaki-brown body plumage for brilliant yellow. Male Lesser and Lawrence's Goldfinches are not as gaudy but remain equally bright year round. The Pine Siskin is a small brownish bird with a yellow stripe across the wing, most easily visible in flight. These birds are often seen in large flocks and are common backyard birds throughout most of their range.

WHERE THEY LIVE: Weedy open fields and roadsides, particularly with sunflowers or thistles, woodland edges.

WHAT THEY EAT: Seeds of thistles, dandelions, and other members of the sunflower family, grass seeds, small tree seeds (birch, alder), buds, young leaves, small fruits, insects.

SOUNDS: High pitched trills and twitters, plaintive chirps. Pine Siskins have an accelerating rising trill like a thumbnail drawn over a comb.

ETC.: Goldfinches and siskins are closely related to the domestic canary and are sometimes called "wild canaries."

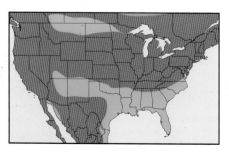

● Range of goldfinches and siskins in summer.
● Range of goldfinches and siskins in winter.
● Range where goldfinches and siskins are found all year.

Opposite: Lawrence's Goldfinch. ***Above:*** Male American Goldfinch. ***Above inset:*** Female American Goldfinch.

Old World Sparrows No. of species: 2

SIZE: 6 inches

HOW TO KNOW THEM: One of our most common urban birds, the bird we know as the House Sparrow or "English Sparrow" is an introduced species from Europe and is not closely related to North American sparrows. They are large brown birds with shorter legs, thicker bills, and less musical voices than native sparrows.

WHERE THEY LIVE: House Sparrows are common in urban areas throughout North America and the world. They seem more at home in the city and suburbs than in any rural, natural setting. The Eurasian Tree Sparrow, a related species, has become established around St. Louis.

WHAT THEY EAT: Anything from insects and seeds to pet food to discarded french fries.

SOUNDS: Non-musical chirps.

ETC.: The House Sparrow was one of only two unqualified successes among the many attempts by fans of Shakespeare to introduce all the birds mentioned in his plays to the United States. Ironically, native populations in Britain have declined as a result of increased use of pesticides and other changes in agriculture.

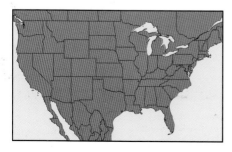

● **Range where old world sparrows are found all year.**

Opposite: Female House Sparrow. **Above:** Male House Sparrow.

Index

Selected Bibliography

Below is a select list of books and websites that provide useful information about birds. Each of the books was selected not just for the quality of information it provides, but for its currency—every one was published after 1995.

BOOKS

Baumann, Mel M., ed. *National Geographic Reference Atlas to the Birds of North America*. Washington, D.C.: National Geographic Society, 2003.

Elphick, Jonathan, ed. *Atlas of Bird Migration: Tracing the Great Journeys of the World's Birds*. New York: Random House, 1995.

Field Guide to the Birds of North America, 4th edition. Washington, D.C.: National Geographic Society, 2002.

Kaufman, K. *Lives of North American Birds*. Boston: Houghton Mifflin Co., 1996.

Peterson, Roger Tory. *A Field Guide to Eastern Birds*, 5th edition. Boston: Houghton Mifflin Co., 2001.

Sibley, David A. *The Sibley Guide to Bird Life & Behavior*. New York: Alfred A. Knopf, 2001.

Weidensaul, Scott. *Living on the Wind: Across the Hemisphere With Migratory Birds*. New York: North Point Press, 2000.

WEBSITES

American Bird Conservancy. www.abcbirds.org

American Birding Association. www.americanbirding.org

The Birds of North America Online. http://bna.birds.cornell.edu/

Photographic Credits